Published by
Kandour Ltd.
1-3 Colebrooke Place
London
N1 8HZ
UNITED KINGDOM

This edition printed in 2006
for Bookmart Ltd
Registered Number 2372865
Trading as Bookmart Ltd
Blaby Road
Wigston
Leicester LE18 4SE

First published 2006

10 9 8 7 6 5 4 3 2 1

Author: Jack M. Driver
Editor: Michael Vaughn
Design and Layout: George Georgiou
Production: Karen Lomax
Jacket Design: George Georgiou & Christian Nichols

Printed and Bound in China

ISBN 10: 1-904756-91-3

ISBN 13: 978-1-904756-91-0

THE VATICAN

CONSPIRACIES, CODES,
AND THE
CATHOLIC CHURCH

Jack M. Driver

Kandour Ltd

CONTENTS

chapter 1

In Dan Brown's "Angels and Demons", Harvard Professor of Symbology Robert Langdon and Vittoria Vetra, "a beautiful and mysterious Italian scientist" are granted access to the dusty vaults of the Vatican Archives.

The Manuscript

shrouded in secrecy. But it's all there in the archives of the Vatican, including the admission of a prominent Jesuit confessor of witches, Father Frederick von Spee, that he was convinced of the innocence of every women he met before her execution.

And what of the many spies that the Vatican had employed over the course of the years, such as Abbe de Salamon, the official intelligence agent in Paris of Pope Pius VI?

During the French Revolution, when the Church was under attack from the forces of secularization, he mingled with the masses in disguise eavesdropping in shops and loosening tongues in taverns with rounds of drinks. By night he organized his network of trusted couriers from his hiding place under a kiosk in the Bois de Boulogne, sending information back to the Vatican.

At a dangerous time for the clergy when hundreds of priests were massacred, he risked his life to keep the lines of communication open with Rome as the official channels were being watched. At one point he was even arrested and imprisoned but used his gift of the gab to talk his way out!

Or spymaster Francesco Cappaccini, who kept the Vatican informed about anti-Catholic plotters in Belgium

This rare privilege is bestowed so they can hunt for clues to foil an Illuminati plot to blow up the Vatican and they do indeed find an obscure manuscript by Galileo Galilei, which points the way to follow in the killer's footsteps.

It is a shame however that they are in such a hurry, as the seconds are steadily ticking away, because they would have found much to interest them in this historical treasure trove, unrivalled anywhere in the world.

Take for instance the records of the Inquisition, which according to recent research may have sent over 30,000 people in the seventeenth century alone to a slow and agonizing death at the stake. Those who were found guilty were often entirely ignorant of the charges against them, the identity of the witnesses and the case of the prosecution

and Holland, who were stirring up trouble in the Papal States. His genius for code-breaking had been put to good use in the papal secretariat of state, where he brought the Vatican up to date with modern espionage tactics. He persuaded Pope Leo

The French Revolution

Bois de Boulogne

with modern espionage tactics. He persuaded Pope Leo XII to abandon the hopelessly out-of-date fixed substitution cipher in favor of the polyalphabetical systems pioneered by the cryptographer Matteo Argenti and the polymath Leon Alberti, who could apparently "with feet tied, leap over a standing man; could in the great cathedral throw a coin far up to the ring against the vault; and amuse himself by taming wild horses and climbing mountains!"

Through his agents within the royal court of the House of Orange, Cappacini was able to trace the source of a great deal of inflammatory anti-Vatican literature that was spreading dissent and sowing the seeds of revolution in the Papal States. No doubt with an array of devices for inflicting the most excruciating pain, at his disposal, he persuaded one of those he arrested to become a double agent and thus he was able to eradicate a wide network of revolutionaries.

More recently, the arts of subterfuge were directed inwards against those within the Church who espoused the theories of modernism. Many of the younger clergy wanted to incorporate the discoveries of the new scientific methods into their studies. Critical evaluation of the bible had shown, for example, that there was more than one author in several

of the Gospels and passages had been added many years after they were first compiled. Geological research had already proven that the world was far older than the few thousand years given in the Book of Genesis. There were new calls to replace the strict literal reading of the bible with a metaphorical interpretation but this was anathema to Pius X and he issued an encyclical Pascendi formally condemning 65 propositions of modernism and denouncing all tendencies which aimed at a reform of dogma.

His chief spymaster was the prelate Umberto Benigni, who was well-versed in modern communication systems from his early days running newspapers and a news service. He used his knowledge to develop an extensive intelligence network, and it seems no one was safe. Thousands of informers spied on each other, reporting back to Benigni's office in Rome if they had so much as overheard a suspicious phrase or seen a priest with a book other than the bible in his hands.

In an atmosphere resembling a Stalinist purge, there was no right of appeal, dismissals were instantaneous,

Pope Pius X

neither the names of the witnesses nor the charges were revealed and even those attempting to clear the name of their brethren were found guilty by association.

The situation soon got out of hand and Benigni became isolated and paranoid accusing everyone around him, even at the highest echelons of the Vatican, of modernism.

In one instance his zeal against "the enemy from within" was so misguided that he worked to deny a Christian burial to an English modernist, Father George Tyrrell.

With Pius X's death in 1914, the prevailing mood of the Church changed and Benigni became an embarrassing anachronism. He ended up spying for the Russians, but thanks to his campaign the Vatican entered the second decade of the twentieth century seriously lagging behind the rest of the world in its knowledge of the latest academic advances.

However one thing the Vatican still excelled in was diplomatic espionage and this proved extremely useful during World War II when it found itself entirely at the mercy of the dictator Mussolini, who could express his displeasure by withholding water and electricity from the sovereign City State.

Pius XII had to play a complicated game to ensure the Vatican kept its independence and he was able to keep his diplomatic channels open with a sophisticated code known only as "Green", which is still a mystery to modern cryptographers.

The Nazi Flag

Thanks to this unbroken cipher, the Vatican was able to warn the Belgians and the Netherlands in 1940 that Hitler was about to invade. It was also used when Pius XII liased between the British Government and a group of renegade German officers who wanted clearance that if they assassinated Hitler, the British would seek a peaceful settlement of the war.

Unfortunately for those who were yet to die the plot failed because the conspirators were not deemed capable of unifying the German forces.

During the war, parts of the Vatican itself were used to hide Jewish refugees and many priests risked their lives providing safe-houses and bolt-holes for the enemies of the Nazis. Such commendable actions are often forgotten amid all the talk of the Vatican's part in organizing ratlines for

Mussolini

Nazi war crime suspects fleeing to South America.

If the rumors are to be believed, the Vatican's involvement with international espionage continued right into the 1980s. Marco Politi and Carl Bernstein assert in their biography of Pope John Paul II that he used his secret diplomatic channels to help the CIA keep track of Soviet troop maneuvers and donated over $30 million to the Polish Union Solidarity to fund his homeland's peaceful resistance to the Soviet Union.

Dan Brown's tale of murder in the Vatican may also not be as far-fetched as it might at first seem. For as recently as 1998, two of the Swiss Guards and a woman were gunned down within the walls of the Vatican City. The Commander Alois Estermann, his wife and a young lance corporal Cedric Tornay were found riddled with bullets. Within a very short

Pioneer of the Swiss Guards in France, 1779 -
Sapeur Gardes Suisses

space of time, with the whiff of a cover-up in the air, the Vatican had concluded that Tornay had shot the couple and then turned the gun on himself "in a fit of madness."

Cardinal Sodano swore the Swiss Guards to secrecy and waited for the dust to settle. However an independent inquiry uncovered a murky tale of ambition, bullying and sexual rivalry, with an Opus Dei member thrown in to add spice to the story, but there were no clear answers.

John Follain, in his detailed investigation "City of Secrets", was moved to write: "Even today, the conspiracy of silence and the refusal to admit any responsibility prevails. The Vatican's inquiry remains closed, the files still locked away."

In several instances of violence within the Vatican the Popes themselves were the victims. The first to be assassinated was Pope John VIII, poisoned by his entourage and then clubbed to death because the poison was taking too long to work! In the time of the Borgias nothing could be taken for granted, not even an innocuous fig or appetizing melon. Powdered glass was almost a staple

SAPEUR DES   GARDES SUISSES

food and Pope Alexander VI succumbed to arsenic in his wine. Almost immediately his flesh turned black and his tongue swelled to an enormous size. Indeed his body became so bloated with gas that the lid to his coffin could not be closed, without the undertakers first jumping up and down on it!

But even the Popes of the twentieth century were not immune from the assassin's blade. Pius XI, who had originally supported Mussolini but then turned against him, was widely rumored to have been dispatched with a contaminated syringe by Mussolini's daughter's lover.

And in the seventies there were dark mutterings that Pope Paul VI had been replaced with an impostor, by three powerful cardinals, because of his socialist tendencies. Five years after his death, reports were circulating that the real Pope was alive and well living in a suburb of Rome under an assumed identity. Photographs from before and after were compared, which seemed to confirm that the eyes and ears were markedly different.

Perhaps the most sensational tale told about the Vatican is that one of the Popes was in fact a woman. This story, which was doing the rounds as early as the 13th century, involves a rather androgynous woman, who by dint of her intelligence and ambition, managed not only to pass herself off as a man, but eventually landed the top job itself. According to the Dominican chronicler Jean de Mailly, she went riding one day and the stress caused her to give birth to a premature child, whereupon she was tied to a horse's tail, dragged through the streets of Rome and stoned to death by an angry mob.

Ultimately, conspiracy theorists will take you as far as you want to go. The internet is full of websites, some of them

Rosary and Bible

Titanic

espousing very unsound ideological views, which blame the Jesuits for just about every event in the last five hundred years, even going so far as to link the sinking of the Titanic to a conspiracy to thwart the World Bank!

In these pages you will find a more sober assessment of the codes and conspiracies of the Catholic Church, which is no less entertaining though based on fact.

However this book should not be taken as a critique of the Roman Catholic faith, rather it should be read as an examination of the way that an institution as powerful as the Vatican can sometimes become distracted by the trappings of that power and dissipate its energy in the maintenance of its status, to the detriment of the original purpose for which it was founded.

The worst excesses of the most notorious Popes are long gone but they should never be forgotten. Being entrusted with the mission to spread the word of Christ was after all a responsibility and not a right.

chapter 2

Shortly after the end of World War II, in December 1945, an Egyptian peasant named Muhammad Ali al-Samman was digging for bir lime underneath the cliff tops of the Jabal al-Tarif mountain range, when he stumbled across an earthenware jar that contained thirteen leather-bound papyrus scrolls or codices.

Grail

Although some of these books were thrown on the fire by the peasant's mother and thus are lost forever, the remainder of the collection found its way through smugglers and dealers to the appropriate academic experts who set about translating them from the Coptic language used by Egyptian Christians from the early Christian era until about the eighth century AD.

What emerged was an astoundingly different picture of early Christianity to the orthodox presentation we have come to accept through the established Gospels of the Canon. Scholars date the scrolls at around 350 AD but the texts are copies of much earlier documents. We know from the writings of Irenaeus, the Bishop of Lyons, that some of these alternative gospels may have been around as early as 150 AD and crucially one or two may even predate the Gospels of the New Testament. Thus it is just possible that some are based on eye-witness accounts and the testimony

Jesus carrying the Cross

of the men and women who were present during the last days of Jesus Christ's life.

Among the many startling revelations from the Nag Hammadi Gospels are the words reputedly spoken by Christ himself in the "Second Treatise of the Great Seth" in which he claims not to have died on the cross:

"I did not succumb to them as they had planned. And I did not die in reality but in appearance, lest I be put to shame by them. For my death which they think happened, happened to them in their error and blindness, since they

nailed their man unto their death. It was another, their father, who drank the gall and the vinegar; it was not I. They struck me with the reed; it was another, Simon, who bore the cross on his shoulder. It was another upon whom they placed the crown of thorns. And I was laughing at their ignorance."

And in the Gospel of Mary, there seems to be some kind of dispute between Mary Magdalene and Peter the Apostle. "Sister" he asks her. "We know that the Savior loved you more than the rest of women. Tell us the words of the Savior which you remember, which you know but we do not."

In reply to Peter's angry questions "Did he really speak privately with a woman and not

openly to us? Are we to turn about and all listen to her? Did he prefer her to us?" another unnamed disciple replies: "Surely the Savior knows her very well. That is why he loved her more than us."

The Gospel of Philip leaves no room for doubt as to the relationship between Jesus and Mary:

"And the companion of the Savior is Mary Magdalene. But Christ loved her more than all the disciples and used to kiss her often on the mouth. The rest of the disciples were offended by it and expressed disapproval. They said to him, "Why do you love her more than all of us?" The Savior answered and said to them, "Why do I not love you like her?"

These and other similar passages have shed a whole new light on the life of the man who, millions of people

Mary Magdalene

Leonardo da Vinci

around the world believe was the Son of God. Biblical studies have been taken down a new avenue, which has culminated in two phenomenal best-sellers, "The Holy Blood and the Holy Grail" and "The Da Vinci Code."

Everyone it seems, from the milkman to the major-general, knows about the theory that Mary Magdalene had a relationship with Jesus Christ and bore him a child. According to the same theory the legend of the Holy Grail, (which can both refer to the cup in which Joseph of Arimethia caught the blood of Christ as it spilled from his side and the cup from which Jesus drank at the Last Supper), in French "San Greal", is actually a misunderstanding or a deliberate concealment of "Sang Real" meaning "Holy Blood."

So why has such an astounding revelation, "the most shattering secret of the last two thousand years" as the publicizers of the Baigent, Leigh and Teabing book put it, remained just that, a secret when it seems to have been a widely held belief in the first few centuries of this era?

The answer is that a propaganda campaign was launched by the fathers of the Church to whitewash this heresy from the pages of history and so effective was it, that it disappeared from public knowledge for nearly two thousand years.

The dangers that these heretical teachings posed to the Orthodox Church were manifold. Firstly there was the issue of power and authority.

Many of the so-called Gnostic schools of Christianity promoted a dualist cosmology. On the one hand there was the realm of the Spirit, from which the Word, Light, Love and Truth derive and on the other hand was Matter, the Fallen World, Corruption and Decay. If Jesus was incarnated he belonged to the World of Matter and thus could not be the Son of God because the two states were irreconcilable. Therefore they believed that he was a divinely inspired

prophet, but not in and of himself divine.

The poet and Gnostic teacher Valentinus born in Egypt around 110 AD went even further, proposing a metaphysical system in which the God of the Old Testament is an inferior Demiurge, rather low in the cosmological hierarchy and jealously guarding the truth from mankind.

In the Valentinian system there were three types of man: carnal types whose obsession with the material plane precluded all chance of salvation, psychic types who can attain salvation by imitation of the Christ (an eternal archetype of the cosmos) and pneumatic types, who have the divine spirit within them and, although they may not know it, are superior to the Demiurge.

Now as soon as heretical teachings that Jesus Christ was a mere mortal begin to take hold, the authority of the Church is deeply shaken for suddenly they no longer hold the keys to the gates of the Kingdom of Heaven. It is one thing to say that you hold your spiritual authority in a direct line of papal succession through Saint Peter from the Son of God himself. Then you may justly expect the mightiest emperors to make obeisance and seek your blessing. It is quite another to be the mere keeper of a body of wise maxims and practical lore handed down from the mouth of an enlightened and charismatic preacher.

The problem is exacerbated when people start claiming that not only was Jesus a mortal, but he did what most mortals do by marrying and having children. Then the Church is faced with the prospect of having to fight a rearguard action against claims that the true inheritance of Jesus is not to be found in the papal line through Peter but must be sought in the bloodline through Mary Magdalene.

Perhaps even more dangerous to the authority of the Church was the emphasis on Gnosis promoted in many of the heretical schools in the first centuries after the birth of Christ. Gnosis was direct knowledge of the spiritual source of creation which could be attained through ritual and initiation into the secret "mysteries." This involved rigorous self-examination and a purification of the soul by turning away from the temptations and concerns of the material world and focussing the mind on the spiritual plane.

Naturally this was extremely worrying for the Church. Gnostic schools promised direct knowledge of God, bypassing the need for faith, which the Church held in such esteem and completely removing the need for the Church hierarchy, which hitherto was supposed to intercede on one's behalf.

Iranaeus, the Bishop of Lyon, was the first to launch a counter-attack against the Gnostics. In his enormous five-volume work "A Refutation and Subversion of

Gnostics

Knowledge Falsely So called" written around 180 AD he struck the first blow, deliberately severing the link between Gnosticism and Christianity, emphasizing the pagan roots of Gnosticism, a paganism which Christ had come to sweep away.

Irenaeus realized that in order for the Church to survive it had to discourage the kind of questioning and search for truth that Gnosis involved. Therefore it was necessary to establish a fixed doctrine which was to be taken on faith. With this in mind he examined the available works on Christianity, a mammoth task in itself, discarding those texts which did not meet with his requirements and including those which did. Thus he arrived at the Canon which we know today as the New Testament.

For Irenaeus and the Church leaders who followed in his wake, Christ had accomplished the only creative act necessary for fallen man by the miracle of the Resurrection and all that was needed by good Christians was an endless celebration of his life by partaking in the Eucharist. Intellectual speculation was not only unnecessary it was potentially very dangerous.

Here we have an essential and irreconcilable gulf between the Gnostics and the adherents of Orthodoxy. The Gnostics were lovers of knowledge, to the extent that certain sects identified themselves with the symbol of the serpent for its role in freeing mankind from the bondage imposed upon them by the God of the Old Testament. According to them Jehovah was a jealous god, a Demiurge, who had not created the Earth and the Heavens but was rather created himself to organize them. Unaware of his own low cosmological status and afraid of mankind, he kept Adam in a state of ignorance until the serpent brought about his Gnosis.

The Church Fathers on the other hand reviled the serpent and equated Adam's Gnosis with a fall from Grace.

Iranaeus, the Bishop of Lyon

Council of Nicaea

For them, the serpent's act was a diabolical act of wickedness that could only have come from Satan himself.

In those days nothing ever happened quickly and Church unity took a long time to coalesce. By the fourth century however the cement was starting to hold and in 325 AD the Council of Nicaea was attended by over three hundred bishops from across the widespread Christian community. The Nicene Creed as it became known established once and for all a fixed statement of accepted Christian orthodoxy.

Whereas beforehand, the bishops might have tried to argue the heretics round to their point of view, Christianity had now become welded to the might of the Roman Empire and where pleading failed force would prevail.

The emperor Constantine had converted to a sun-worshipping cult known as "Sol Invictus", which in all respects was a traditionally pagan religion, with the vital exception that it was monotheistic. As it considered other deities to be aspects of the solar divinity it was unusually tolerant and thus Christianity flourished. Constantine was also concerned with unity and stability across his empire and he was fully aware that a universal religion could achieve this. And so he fused Sol Invictus, Mithraism and Christianity.

So for example, whereas Christians had sanctified Saturday as the Sabbath in accordance with Jewish tradition, they moved the day to the "Venerable Day of the Sun", on which Constantine had ordered the law courts to close. Similarly,

St. Constantine summoned the bishops
of the Christian Church to Nicaea

they moved the birthday of Jesus Christ, which prior to the fourth century had been celebrated on January 6th to December 25th, which was the festival of the Natalis Invictus, the Winter Solstice when the Sun loosens the land from the icy grip of Winter and the days grow longer.

It was Constantine who called the Council of Nicaea at which power was consolidated in the hands of the bishops. He authorized the seizure of heretical writings, which challenged the unity he sought. Crucially he financed the writing of new copies of the bible. As Diocletian, a pagan emperor and vociferously anti-Christian, had ordered the destruction of all documents relating to the life of Christ found anywhere within the Roman empire, this gave the new proponents of the orthodox Church a chance to literally re-write the bible.

The whitewash was nearly complete.

Let us now travel forward in time some nine hundred years and move the location to the south of France, the Languedoc to be precise. The year is 1209 and some 30,000 warriors have descended from Northern Europe to slaughter the local inhabitants and raze the towns and cities to the ground, all with the Church's blessing.

During what has become known as the Albigensian Crusade, in the town of Beziers alone, over 15,000 men, women and children were put to the sword. Immediately before this bloodthirsty massacre the commander of the army asked the representative of the Church in Rome how to distinguish the heretics so that the good Christians might be spared. He replied,

"Kill them all. God will recognize His own."

He later boasted to the Pope "neither age nor sex nor status was spared."

What was so dangerous about the Albigenses or Cathars as they are also known, that prompted the Pope to call for a crusade within Christendom, promising

remission of all sins and a guaranteed place in Heaven, to all who would don the tunic with the emblazoned crucifix and take up the sword? What prompted this holy war lasting nearly forty years, in which Dominic Guzman so zealously pursued the heretics that he would be rewarded by the founding of the Dominican Order, which would play such a vital role in the establishment of the Holy Roman and Universal Inquisition?

The region of the Languedoc was an independent principality with an incredibly advanced culture, similar in many ways to Byzantium. Whereas much of the European aristocracy was illiterate, concerned only with land and property and the power that accrued therefrom, the nobility of the Languedoc were well versed in the liberal arts, and were familiar with Arabic advances in mathematics, and Jewish schools of mysticism.

Unusually for the time, women enjoyed high status within society and the notion of courtly love was celebrated by troubadours. At a time when they were seen as little better than chattels, child-bearing commodities that could be bought and sold, many of the high positions in the Cathar Church were occupied by women.

As well as a high regard for the feminine principle (which will become important later!) the Cathars denied the divinity of Christ. It seemed that the Gnostic schools of the early first millennium had survived the attempts to stamp them out and resurfaced centuries later in southern France.

Their essentially dualist outlook could not be reconciled with a Son of God who incarnated into the physical world and partook of matter, which they believed was created by an evil entity they called Rex Mundi, or King of the World. As such Jesus could only ever be a purely spiritual being or a mortal prophet who died for his principles.

This was clearly unacceptable to the Holy See and when it became likely that Catharism would become the dominant religion in Languedoc due to the apathy and corruption of the local Roman clergy and was in danger of spreading to the major urban centers in Europe, a decision was made to crush the "foul leprosy of the South."

As with the suppression of the Templars by the Catholic Church a smear campaign preceded the use of force, and once again charges of "unnatural sexual practices" reverberated in the European corridors of power. On January 14th, 1208, the

Cathars being expelled

Church of Rome got the excuse it needed to act, when one of the Papal Legates to the Languedoc was murdered. Although there was no evidence of Cathar involvement, the Church mobilized the Northern European nobility who stood to make enormous financial gains by plundering this wealthy region.

Over the next thirty years every single Cathar town fell except for the mountain fortress of Montsegur. During the course of the crusade, rumors began to spread amongst the Northern invaders of the fabulous wealth of the Cathars. As their religion forbade the bearing of arms, they had paid mercenaries to fight their cause. How had they kept up these payments for thirty years? Did the money come from the Languedoc nobility, many of whom had converted to Catharism?

There were also stories about the legendary wealth of the Visigoths, who had sacked Rome in 410 AD and carried back to southern France everything of value from the city including the treasure of the Temple of Solomon, which had in turn been carried away by the Romans in AD 70 when Jerusalem was razed to the ground. According to legend, contained in the spoil was the Ark of the Covenant itself. Another story going around was that the Merovingian King Dagobert had married a Visigoth princess and much of the wealth had passed to him and had been kept at nearby Rennes-le-Chateau (more of this later!)

When the Inquisitors offered reasonable terms to the defenders of Montsegur, promising a full pardon to the mercenaries and only a mild penance to any "parfaits" (high priests) who would recant their heresy, the Cathars asked for two weeks to consider the terms. At the end of the truce, some twenty of the fighting men had converted to Catharism and the other two hundred or so declared they would not recant.

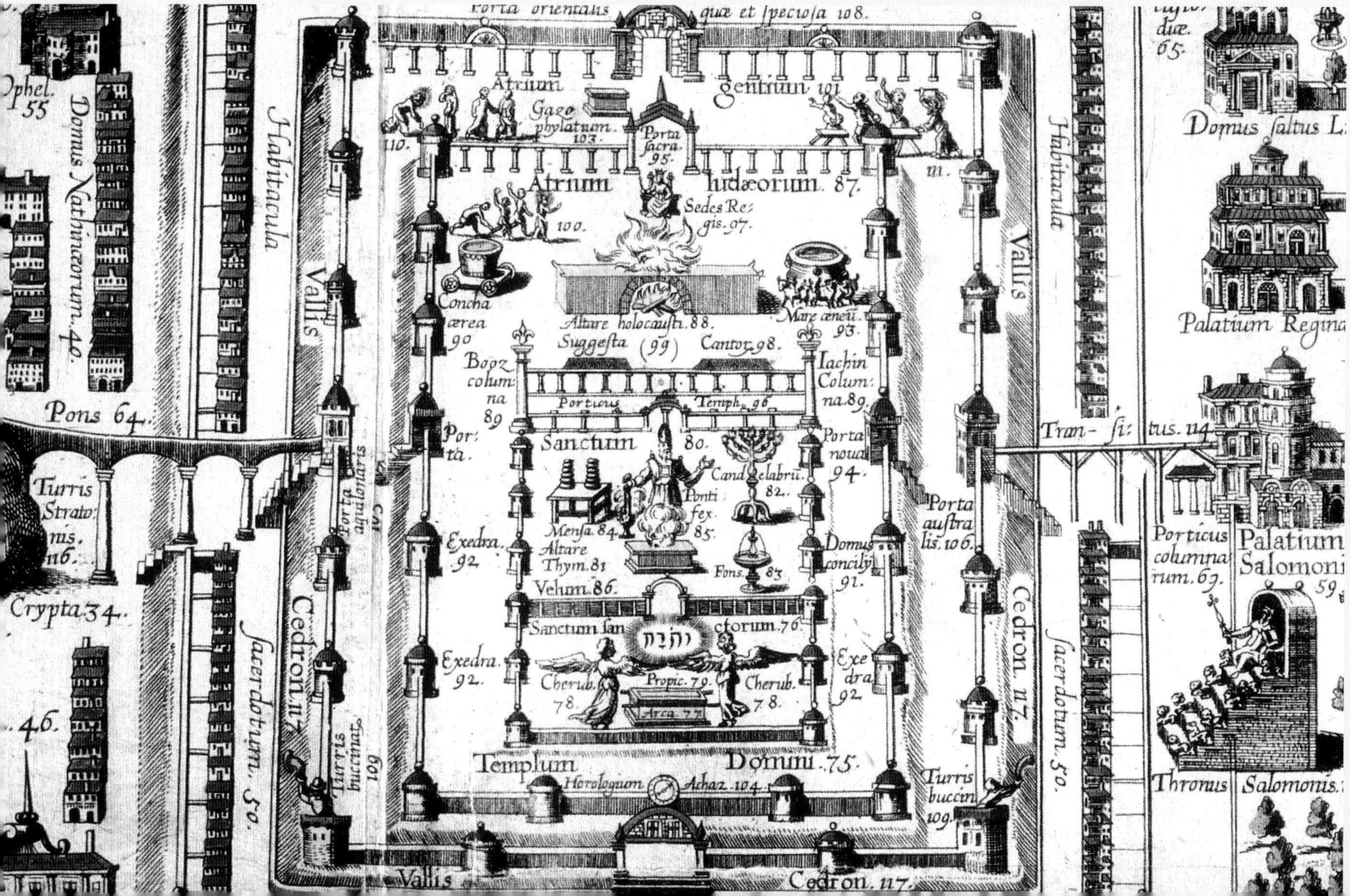

Temple of Solomon

As they had voluntarily given up hostages to guarantee the truce, they had to open up the gates to the invaders and the parfaits were dragged outside to the awaiting Inquisition. Because there was no time to construct a stake for each sinner, they were all burned together in a large stockade filled with wood while their comrades looked on.

When the troops poured into the citadel, every single one of them had only thing on his mind: finding the Cathar treasure. However despite tearing the place apart in their lust for gold, they didn't find so much as a measly little trinket. Gossip spread around the camp. Where was the fabled gold? Had they hidden it? Had it been stolen? And then they began to consider the geography of the location.

The fortress stood atop a huge rocky outcrop with sheer cliff faces on several sides. The besiegers numbered upwards of ten thousand but even with such a large force they had not quite managed to make their ring around the mountain absolutely watertight and it was possible that some of the Cathars had been able to bribe their way through by paying off local mercenaries sympathetic to their cause. Indeed this is the only explanation for their having been able to withstand the siege for so long. Rumor piled up on hearsay until one consistent story was being touted as the explanation. Under threat of torture, several local soldiers revealed that they had been bribed to turn a blind eye as four Cathars let themselves down the sheer western face of the mountain using ropes and carrying no more than light packs on their backs. Once on the ground they had disappeared into the night and were never seen again.

It was clear that if this story was true the Cathars were carrying no significant quantities of treasure, for the simple reason that they would not have been able to carry a hoard big enough to make the risk worthwhile.

Troops looting Cathar treasure

Conjecture arose as to what could have been so precious and yet light enough to carry in knapsacks. The answer was there for anyone with wit enough to make the leap of imagination that treasure does not necessarily have to mean gold and silver but can be knowledge, preserved perhaps in bundles of parchment.

Here the two strands come together. Firstly, the Cathar's insistence on the mortality of Jesus Christ and secondly the Catholic Church's fanatical zeal to make sure every last Cathar was wiped off the face of the earth. The question that begs itself is, did the Cathars have proof of something that the Holy See would do anything to conceal, going so far as to break the Lord's commandment not to kill?

This is also where the Holy Order of Warrior Monks known as the Knights Templar comes in. Rivalling the Cathars in mystery and romanticism, they were also brutally suppressed by the Catholic Church, little over half a century after the Albigensian Crusade. For a detailed look at the orthodox version of why they were hunted to extinction, see the separate chapter devoted to them. There is another version however, beloved by Holy Grail enthusiasts.

The theory rests on the fact that when the Order was founded in 1118, the original nine members were invited to quarter themselves in one of the wings of the royal palace on the Temple Mount, the site of the Temple of Solomon. Beneath their billet were the "Stables of Solomon", big enough apparently to hold two thousand horses. It was here that the Templars were rumored to have begun extensive excavations.

The Templar Order grew immensely wealthy very rapidly. The explanation favored by academic historians for this exponential accumulation of wealth, is that it rested on donations by the nobility and the development of banking, based on their trustworthiness and proven ability to secure their safety deposits.

The other explanation is that they discovered something beneath the Temple Mount. It is possible that there was some treasure left after the Romans looted the

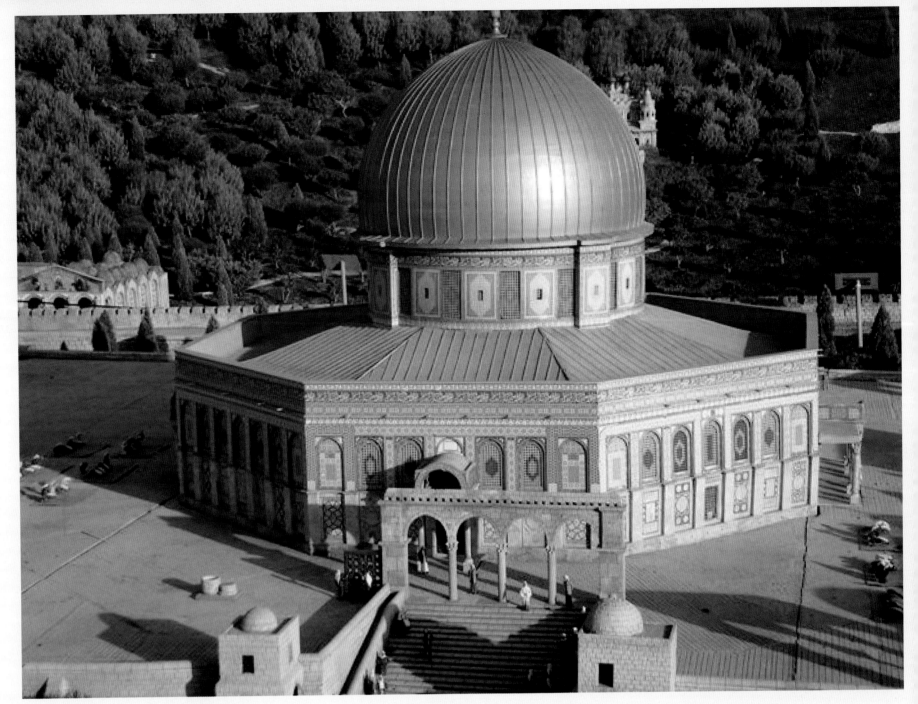

Temple Mount

Temple in AD 70. But again we are faced with the conclusion that perhaps the treasure was knowledge. Knowledge of something so important that an institution such as the Catholic Church was prepared at first to pay to ensure that knowledge was kept secret but then perhaps tired of shelling out, ruthlessly exterminated the Templars to make certain the secret would die with them. There are after all two ways to deal with a blackmailer. You either pay up, and face the prospect of paying for the rest of your life or you take the decision to silence the blackmailer, by whatever means you deem necessary.

The location in which they were digging does lead to the intriguing possibility that perhaps the Temple priests, unable to prevent the ransacking of the sacred site by the Romans, hid something of great importance to them close at hand, knowing full well the soldiers would only have eyes for the gold.

Whatever secret the Templars had discovered it appeared to have disappeared with them, as they took great care to destroy all their records before they could fall into the wrong hands. However when we examine the charges brought against the Templars and used to whip up public opinion against them, charges that have always been thought to be false, if we suppose for a moment that they were true, we see an echo of a familiar heresy.

The most heinous charge was that of spitting and trampling on the cross. To a Christian nothing could be more repugnant. But what if this were part of a ritual of a cult that did not believe that Christ died on the cross? Then it would be a symbolic act of contempt for a belief they thought naïve and foolish. And if they thought Christ was not the Son of God, but a mortal prophet, this could easily be turned to the Church's advantage, by associating the denial of Christ with the embrace of the Devil. Some of the confessions drawn from Templar knights under torture do not chime with the image of idol worship levelled against the Order but rather seem indicative of Gnostic principles. The fact that they weren't over embellished to look like admissions of Satanism suggests they are genuine.

One knight claimed he was told upon initiation, "Do not believe that the man Jesus whom the Jews crucified in Outremer is God and can save you." Another was shown a crucifix and told "Set not much faith in this, for it is too young." Yet another was told, "You believe wrongly, because Christ is indeed a false prophet. Believe only in God in heaven, and not in him."

The notion that Christ was a false prophet was more common than we might think nowadays, given that history is written by the victors. Two sects in particular, the Johanites and the Mandaeans, held that Saint John the Baptist was the real Messiah. This is particularly relevant

St John The Baptist

given the important role that Saint John the Baptist and Saint John the Evangelist play in Freemasonry, which may well represent a modern resurgence of the beliefs and rituals of the Templars that survived underground after being broken up by the Catholic Church.

But the connection with the Cathars goes even deeper. The fourth Grandmaster of the Templars, Bertrand de Blanchefort, was a nobleman with distinct Cathar sympathies and his ancestral seat in the Languedoc lay only a few miles from their stronghold at Montsegur. It is also

highly probable that there were many Cathars within the
Order itself. Joining the Templars and
risking one's life to protect pilgrims
on their way to the Holy Land was
deemed so noble by the Church as
to absolve any sin, even heresy and
during the Albigensian Crusade
many noblemen were given the
choice of doing such a penance rather
than facing death.

Bertrant de
Blanchefort
Seal

A few years after his appointment as Grandmaster,
de Blanchefort imported a crew of German-speaking miners
to the area around Rennes-le-Chateau, which is about half a
day's ride from Montsegur. According to reports the miners
were kept apart from the local community and watched with
great care by Templar guards. The language barrier seems
purposefully to have been introduced as an extra precaution.
The story was broadcast that they were digging for gold in
the Roman-era gold mines but it was common knowledge
that all the gold had been thoroughly mined many centuries
before.

In the seventeenth century a report was made
by prospectors in the area, who had unearthed evidence
of the German miners' activity. The engineer who wrote
the report was convinced the Germans were not mining.
Either they were excavating a crypt or they were creating a
subterranean vault.

At this point let us examine (as promised!) the goings
on at Rennes-le-Chateau. The long and winding road that
eventually led Baigent, Leigh and Lincoln, the authors
of "Holy Blood and the Holy Grail" to their astounding
conclusions regarding the bloodline of Jesus Christ began
with an investigation into the curious fate of an enigmatic
parish priest, Berenger Sauniere, assigned to the small

Berenger
Sauniere

mountain village of Rennes-le-Chateau in the shadow of
the Pyrenees.

His parish church, dedicated to Mary Magdalene,
stood on the site of a building supposed to date from the time
of the Visigoths in the sixth century. With plenty of time on
his hands in this sleepy village, Sauniere set about some long
overdue restoration work on the church. Underneath the
altar stone were two Visigoth columns, one of which was
hollow. Inside were four parchments rolled up in wooden
cylinders. Two of them contained genealogies and the other
two contained excerpts from the New Testament, but with
the text run together with no word breaks and several letters
made prominent by standing up from the line.

Seeking the guidance of the bishop of Carcassone,
Sauniere was then sent to Abbe Bieil, the Director General

of the Saint Sulpice Seminary in Paris.

Nobody knows what transpired during his three week stay there but by the end he had been introduced to a wide circle of devotees of occult societies, among whom were the composer Claude Debussy and the opera singer Emma Calve who became his lover.

Returning to Rennes-le-Chateau he continued his renovations and on clearing the weeds from the gravestones in the churchyard he discovered an inscription on the headstone of Marie de Blanchefort (of the same house as Bertrand de Blanchefort, the fourth Grandmaster of the Knights Templar) which was an anagram of one of the messages in the concealed parchments.

At this point Sauniere's behavior becomes rather bizarre. He makes extensive tours of the surrounding countryside, collecting geological specimens of rocks and stones. He enters into a correspondence with unknown persons throughout Europe that will see him spending more money per annum on postage stamps than he earns on his meagre stipend. He opens several accounts, one of which is deemed so important by the bank that it

Saint Sulpice Seminary in Paris

sends an official all the way from Paris just to meet with him. In fact by the end of his life he is reckoned to have spent many millions of francs, financing the construction of a road up to the village, a church tower La Tour Magdala and a lavish villa for himself, where he gave sumptuous banquets and received distinguished visitors such as the Secretary of State for Culture and Archduke Johann von Habsburg, the cousin of the Emperor of Austria.

He also funded the complete redecoration of the church and had the words TERRIBILIS EST LOCUS ESTE (THIS PLACE IS TERRIBLE) inscribed over the entrance above a statue of the demon Asmodeus, the guardian of secrets and according to the occult lore of the

Archduke Johann von Habsburg

Caballah, the builder of Solomon's Temple.

Sauniere's extravagant lifestyle began to attract attention within the Church and he was suspended by the bishop of Carcassone, when he refused to divulge the source of his wealth. A tribunal ordered that he be transferred, accusing him of selling indulgences.

Sauniere then went over the bishop's head and either appealed to or threatened the Vatican. The substance of the meeting is not known but he was immediately reinstated and the bishop was warned off by his superiors.

In 1917 Sauniere suffered a massive stroke and a priest was called to his deathbed. When the priest emerged from his bedchamber it transpired that he had refused to perform the last rites because of what Sauniere told him in his final confession. Eyewitnesses described him as trembling and deathly pale. Friends testified that they never saw him smile or laugh again.

When Sauniere's will was read it was discovered that he didn't have so much as a sou to his name. Everything had long ago been transferred to his housekeeper, Marie Denarnaud. She lived on in the villa until after World War II. When the Government later issued a new currency a law was passed to catch out black market profiteers and tax evaders, by which it was necessary to explain how the money was generated. Rather than account for the provenance of the fortune, she piled the money high in the gardens of her villa and set fire to it all.

Selling the villa provided a small income but she was forced to live out her days in very straitened circumstances. She promised Noel Corbu, who had purchased the villa, that before she died she would tell him a secret, which would bring riches and great power. But then she herself suffered a stroke and was struck dumb. Thus she took the secret to her grave.

Nicolas Poussin

The mystery deepens when we learn that Nicolas Poussin's name features in one of the parchments along with the word Bergere (Shepherd). One of Poussin's most famous paintings is entitled "Les Bergeres d'Arcadie" and is widely agreed to show the peak on which Rennes-le-Chateau rests in the background.

In 1656 Abbe Louis Fouquet visited Poussin in Rome and sent a letter back to his brother, the Superintendent of Finances to Louis XIV of France.

"He and I discussed certain things," he wrote "which I shall with ease be able to explain to you in detail, things which will give you advantages which even kings would have great pains to draw from him, and which, according to him, it is possible that nobody else will ever rediscover in the centuries to come. And what is more, these are things so difficult to discover that nothing now on this earth can prove of better fortune nor be their equal."

Unfortunately for Nicolas Fouquet this correspondence was under surveillance and he was arrested and imprisoned soon after receiving the letter. He was kept in total isolation and many historians believe he was the Man in the Iron Mask. Louis XIV went through his entire correspondence himself, no doubt searching for any clues to this great secret. Whatever it was he did not find it, but he eventually managed to acquire the Poussin painting and hung it in his private apartment in Versailles.

The painting shows three shepherds and a shepherdess standing before a tomb, with the inscription "ET IN ARCADIA EGO", literally "And I in Arcadia" presumably meaning that Death is ever-present even in a bucolic scene such as this. The writers of "Holy Blood and the Holy Grail" were puzzled by the absence of a verb until one of the viewers of the BBC program, in which the original research was presented, pointed out that it could be an anagram: "I TEGO ARCANA DEI", "Begone! I conceal the secrets of God."

Louis XIV

Whatever the source of Sauniere's wealth several names keep cropping up: the Merovingian Dynasty, the Knights Templar and the Cathars who were reputed to possess the Holy Grail. During World War II, the Nazis made extensive excavations in the area as part of their search for biblical artefacts such as the Ark of the Covenant and the Spear that pierced Jesus' side as he hung on the cross. They may well have believed that the Holy Grail was hidden somewhere in the environs of Rennes-le-Chateau.

Let us now turn to the Merovingian Dynasty, in particular to Clovis I, the grandson of Merovee who gave his name to the Dynasty. It could be argued that the Roman Church owes its very existence to this Frankish King for he became the defender of the faith when he was converted to Christianity along with 3000 of his warriors after an important victory over the Alamanni tribe.

When the Roman Empire finally fell in 410 AD, Christianity had been the official religion for nearly four generations but without any military muscle behind it, the Latin Church became one of only several competing factions of Christianity, such as the Celtic Church and the Arians, whose claims that Jesus was a mortal prophet were becoming dangerously popular. Let us also not forget the role of the Greek Orthodox Church in Constantinople, which had an often fraught relationship with Rome, much like that between the twentieth century superpowers Russia and America.

As it became apparent that the Merovingian Dynasty was going to be the most powerful force in Western Europe, the leaders of the Roman Church

Clovis I

realized it would be very advantageous to attach themselves to him. His wife's confessor, Saint Remy, liased between Clovis and the Church in Rome, to arrange a deal whereby Clovis would be the head of a Holy Roman Empire.

In return for championing the Roman Church, he was baptized "Novus Constantius", in recognition of his role as successor to the Christian Empire founded under Constantine. With Clovis at its head, this new Holy Roman Empire expanded until much of France and Germany was under its control. The Visigoths, followers of the Arian heresy, were pushed back to, yes! you guessed it, Rennes-le-Chateau, which was then a town with some 30,000 inhabitants.

However on Clovis' death the empire was divided between his four sons and thereafter it became riven with internecine feuds. It looked for a while as though Dagobert II could become the single unifying force that Clovis had been, but he married the niece of the Visigoth King and became sympathetic to the Arian views that she espoused. In fact he made an enemy of the Church of Rome by blocking their attempts to expand on the continent. And so it is almost certain that they colluded with other enemies of his in having him murdered, one of his retainers driving a lance through his eye as he slept.

With his death the Merovingians were finished as a political and military force and the Carolingian dynasty came to the fore, although the first scions were in fact "Mayors of the Palace" to weak Merovingian rulers.

Pepin III appealed to Rome to back his claim to the throne and despite the pact that existed between the Latin Church and the descendants of Clovis I, Rome agreed to make a deal. In an act of public humiliation he cut off King Childeric III's hair, which much like the Nazarites, was said to embody his strength, and had him sequestered in a monastery.

Rome got round the betrayal of the Merovingian bloodline with a cunning forgery. Called "The Donation of Constantine" the document claimed to record an event that occurred at the time of Constantine's conversion to Christianity. Supposedly he gave to the bishop of Rome the symbols of his right to rule, declaring him to be the Vicar of Christ and offering him the throne. The

Childeric III

bishop then gave them back to Constantine, who now ruled on behalf of the bishop, with his permission.

The effect of this document cannot be overstated. Accepted as genuine by the Christian world, it effectively meant that supreme temporal as well as spiritual authority resided in the hands of the Pope who thenceforth became a king-maker. Whereas before, the papacy could only give recognition of a king's right to rule now it could actually confer that power. Thus it was freed from the pact with the Merovingian bloodline and could sanctify the blood of the Carolingian household.

At the first act of coronation bishops in attendance were given a prominence equal to that of the nobility. As for Dagobert II there was a concerted effort to remove all trace of him from the historical records.

The Donation of Constantine

This is where the lines taken by "Holy Blood and the Holy Grail" and "The Da Vinci Code" diverge. In the former, the authors introduce the Priory of Sion as a secret society dedicated to returning the disinherited Merovingian dynasty to the throne. In Dan Brown's book, the Priory of Sion is concerned with a reinstatement of the sacred feminine principle, which was erased from the Christian Church by the male-dominated clergy.

As far as the theory goes that Leonardo da Vinci was once the grandmaster of the Priory of Sion, and alluded to the sacred feminine in his picture of the Last Supper, this is all pure conjecture, the subject of endless heated debate and will perhaps never be resolved. Just when it seemed that the academics had won the day and conclusively proved that the character on Jesus' right hand was the disciple John, albeit rather feminine-looking, computer analysis has shown that the face is an exact replica of a face used to portray Mary in another painting. Of course proving whether someone belongs to a secret society is by its very nature well nigh impossible, given the lengths to which members will go, to preserve their identity from discovery.

The secret dossiers upon which the authors based their research are generally agreed to be twentieth century forgeries, concocted by the enigmatic Pierre Plantard, who seems to have styled himself the true descendent of the Merovingian bloodline.

As for the Church's defamation of Mary Magdalene, there is ample evidence of this. Despite the prominent place even the canonical gospels give her, she was the victim of a deliberate smear campaign by Pope Gregory, whereby her identity was cleverly smudged and fused with that of another Mary so as to paint a portrait of a harlot. And this, in spite of the fact that she was one of only a few of Jesus' followers who dared to be present at his crucifixion. She was also the one who returned to Jesus' tomb to find it empty and it was to her that Jesus first appeared after the resurrection, empowering her to spread the word and hence in effect becoming the first apostle.

Thus even if we ignore the so-called Gnostic Gospels, which the early Church had tried to bury, wherein it is

explicitly stated that Jesus and Mary were lovers and restrict ourselves to the authorized New Testament, we are still faced with the puzzling anomaly of why Mary is accorded so little respect.

In fact at no point do any of the Gospels say that Mary was a prostitute. She is only described as having seven devils cast out of her, which could be a veiled reference to an initiation ceremony. The woman who anoints Jesus' feet is unnamed. She is the one described as a fallen woman but the two have been conflated. There is plenty of evidence to suggest that Mary was in fact a wealthy woman who supported the disciples financially. In Luke she is described as the friend of a dignitary at King Herod's court.

Clearly in its attempt to establish itself as the one true representation of the one true faith, the Catholic Church has worked hard to ensure that Mary's role in Jesus' life is downplayed while simultaneously emphasizing the apostolic succession through Saint Peter, upon which the Church's supremacy was founded.

As to how far their relationship went, Dan Brown is not the first twentieth century writer to speculate that if they were lovers, the most natural thing in the world would have been for them to marry and have children. As early as the 1950s Nikos Kazantzakis wrote "The Last Temptation of Christ", later turned into a film by Martin Scorsese, in which Jesus and Mary were romantically involved.

In fact if Jesus had not been married it would have been worthy of note at least somewhere in the Gospels, so frowned upon was celibacy, except in such ascetic communities as the Essenes. Jewish Mishnaic Law goes far as to state that "an unmarried man may not be a teacher."

Nikos Kazantzakis

If Mary is indeed the woman who anoints Jesus with the spikenard ointment, then she must be very wealthy as in the Gospel of Mark the disciples rebuke her for wasting such costly oil which could have been sold to feed the poor. Wiping Jesus' feet with her hair in a symbolic act of humility would also seem to support the argument that they were married, because to let one's hair down in front of a man who was not one's husband was a very provocative act and could be cited to sue for divorce on the grounds of adultery.

But the Church did such a good job of blackening her name that throughout the middle ages institutions for reformed prostitutes were called Magdalenes.

And so the natural question to ask if we accept the authors' hypothesis that Jesus was married to Mary Magdalene, is what became of her and any children they might have had?

Baigent, Leigh and Lincoln propose that they set sail for southern France and landed in Marseilles. This legend (although without the crucial addition of Mary carrying Jesus' child) can be traced back as early as the beginning of the ninth century to the "Life of Mary Magdalen" by Rabanus. In the legend she is accompanied by Martha, Lazarus and Joseph of Arimathea, who travels on to England

Mary Magdalene

to found a church in Glastonbury, whence arise the legends of King Arthur's court in Camelot and the quest for the Holy Grail.

Southern France may seem like a strange destination for a party of exiles fleeing the Roman occupation of Israel. However, on closer inspection there may well be a connection.

Although in the New Testament she is not described as such, there is considerable weight of circumstantial evidence to support the notion that Mary was a royal member of the tribe of Benjamin. The Dossiers Secrets, purportedly written by the secret society the Priory of Sion, make explicit reference to an incident described in the book of Judges in which a Levite and his concubine are assaulted while enjoying the hospitality of a Benjamite, by men described as "the sons of Belial."

When the other tribes of Israel call for the men to be given up to justice, the Benjamites defend them and are subsequently defeated by the other tribes in battle and made into pariahs. They soon come to lament that one of the twelve tribes has been sundered from the rest but by then many Benjamites have gone into exile.

The Dossiers Secrets state intriguingly that "One day the descendants of Benjamin left their country; certain remained; two thousand years later Godfroi VI de Bouillon became king of Jerusalem and founded the Ordre de Sion."

Was it thus possible that the exiled Benjamites found their way to southern France? And if so, would this explain the proposition that Mary Magdalene travelled there too? Was she in fact heading for a long established community of Jews, of the same house as her own?

The Priory of Sion documents claim that the exiled tribe found their way to Greece, where they intermarried with the Arcadian royal family. By the time of the birth of Christ they had migrated up the Danube and the Rhine, and through dynastic alliance and intermarriage founded the Sicambrian Franks… the immediate ancestors of the Merovingian line!

And so the story comes full circle.

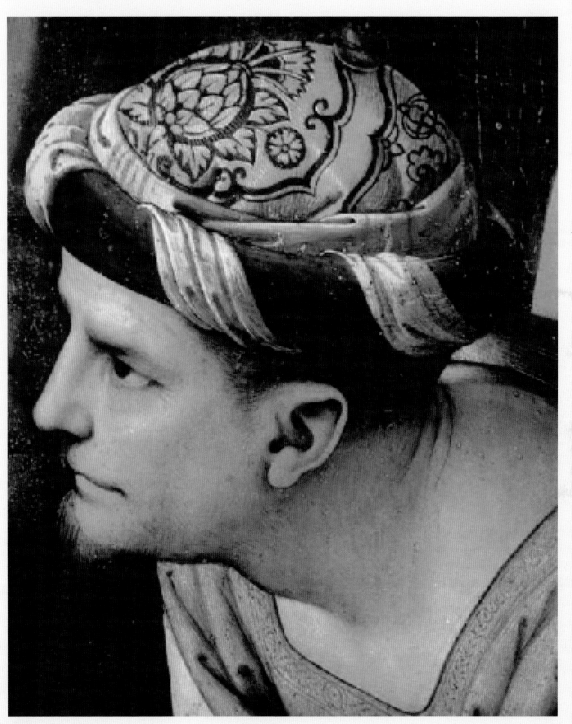

Joseph of Arimathea

There are certainly many Jewish place names in the old Merovingian heartland, such as the villages of Baalon and Avioth and Mount Semita in Lorraine, also known as the Mountain of Sion. There might also be a clue in the legendary founder of the Merovingian dynasty, King Merovee.

According to the myths that are told about him, he had two fathers. While pregnant by her husband, his mother went into the sea to take the weight off her legs and was seduced by a fabulous creature "from beyond the sea." Thus two bloodlines ran in his veins. This myth could well be taken to mean that he received royal blood from his mother, as is the case in Jewish lore, as well as through his Frankish father, King Clodio. Is it also possible that the reference to a divine being from beyond the sea is a veiled reference to a bloodline, which stems from Jesus Christ through Mary Magdalene, arriving on the shores of southern France by ship from Israel?

From then on, Merovingian kings were endowed with occult powers. They were great healers who could speak with animals and they could be identified by their birthmarks, a red cross. Interestingly, this became the emblem of the Templar Knights, who were reputedly the guardians of the Holy Grail.

Indeed the status of the Merovingian kings was so exalted, it seems they were revered in much the same way as the priest-kings of ancient Egypt, that is to say as the mediator between God and his people.

There may also be more to the words "Sang Real" or "Blood Royal" than at first meets the eye. The Gospel of Matthew claims that Jesus, far from being the son of a lowly carpenter, was in fact a direct descendent of the Royal House of David. As such he would have had a legitimate claim to the throne of Palestine.

King David had made Jerusalem his capital, but Jerusalem had actually been apportioned to the tribe of Benjamin, who lost it after their disastrous war. As David had also ousted Saul, the first king of Israel, the Benjamites would not have looked favorably on Jesus' claim to be the King of the Jews. However if he were to align himself with the House of Benjamin by a dynastic alliance, he would have been able to unite the tribes of Israel and as such he would have posed a real threat to the Roman occupying force.

Jesus was born into a period of political turmoil and unrest. Palestine was under military occupation, ruled on behalf of Rome by a series of Arabic puppet kings, of whom Herod was one. The Temple had already been plundered, taxation was at punitive levels and any hint of sedition was brutally put down. Meanwhile rumors abounded of a Messiah who would shake off the yoke of Roman imperial rule and return

King Merovee

King David

the tribes of Israel to their former glory.

The word "Messiah" meant "the anointed one" and had no divine connotations. In particular it referred to one of the lost kings of the line of David who would one day return to free the Israelites from bondage in much the same way as Moses had done.

There is substantial evidence that Jesus deliberately styled himself as this Messiah. For example there was a legend that the Messiah would return in triumph to Jerusalem through the south gate, riding on the back of an ass. This is something Jesus went to great pains to fulfil, telling his disciple to go to Bethany and describing the place where he will find an ass. When he finds everything as Jesus predicted it is taken as some kind of miracle. But is there any need to look for miracles here? Would it not make more sense if Jesus had arranged for the loan of the ass beforehand?

Furthermore it is now generally acknowledged that the bible was slanted to make it more favorable to a

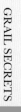

Greco-Roman audience. Therefore the part that the Romans played in Jesus' death was downplayed and the Jews were cast as the villains of the piece.

The very method of Jesus' execution is a punishment reserved exclusively for the enemies of Rome and the idea that the crowd were given a chance to free Jesus by the noble Pontius Pilate (in actual fact a cruel and corrupt governor) but chose instead to free the thief Barabbas has been widely proven to be a complete fabrication, for no such custom existed.

In the early days of Christianity, every effort was made by the Church to establish the divinity of Jesus. Without this crucial factor it would simply have been unable to compete with the other religions with their fantastic and awe-inspiring deities. A humble man admonishing his followers to do unto others as they would have done to themselves and urging them to give up their obsession with material wealth in favor of the spiritual riches in the life to come, was simply not going to cut it in an era characterized by a mystical trend of thought given to bloodthirsty sacrifice and displays of power and glory.

As his deified status gained ground, all connections to his worldly life, especially any descendants he may have sired, became a source of embarrassment. Hence the systematic attempt to erase all trace of them.

Julius Africanus wrote in the third century of relatives of Jesus complaining that their genealogical records had been destroyed, so as to ensure that no subsequent verifiable claim could be made to the throne of David. There were however rumors that some of the records survived the chaos of the uprisings against the Romans, which resulted in the destruction of the Temple.

Were these the same records that the Templars found? Is there a shadowy organization known as the Priory of Sion, which is dedicated to putting the blood descendent of Jesus Christ back on a Europe-wide throne? Is there an equally shadowy element of the Catholic Church dedicated to thwarting such an attempt and to suppress all evidence of Jesus' relationship with Mary Magdalene?

These questions will probably never be answered conclusively and in some ways whether there is any truth in all of it is actually beside the point. As the reviews of "The Da Vinci Code" and "Holy Blood Holy Grail" remind us, this is one of the most fascinating stories ever told.

The Last Supper

chapter 3

ON THE THIRTEENTH DAY OF EACH MONTH BETWEEN MAY AND OCTOBER 1917, AN APPARITION OF THE VIRGIN MARY APPEARED IN THE FIELDS OUTSIDE A REMOTE VILLAGE NEAR FATIMA IN PORTUGAL BEFORE THREE SHEPHERD CHILDREN, LUCIA SANTOS AND HER COUSINS JACINTA AND FRANCISCA MARTO.

The Fatima

According to the children's testimony, she was about the size of a doll and referred to herself as "Our Lady of the Rosary." Lucia described her as "more brilliant than the sun, shedding rays of light clearer and stronger than a crystal glass filled with the most sparkling water."

Hovering over a bush, she imparted three revelations to the children, urging them to do penance and make sacrifices for the many sinners in the world. The only way to bring peace to end World War I, which had already claimed the lives of some of the children's relatives, was to say the Rosary every day.

In response to the apparition's pronouncements, the children fastened ropes around their waists so tightly that they nearly expired with the pain and they went without water on the hottest days of the long dry summer.

This was a time of great uncertainty for the Church in

Lady of Fatima

Portugal, when churches were burnt and priests murdered by Communist revolutionaries and news of the apparition of the Virgin Mary was greeted with rapturous expectation of more miracles to come. Thousands of pilgrims flocked to the village in the hope that she would reappear and the authorities became concerned at the effect it was having on an already tense political situation.

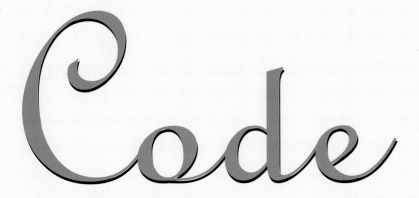

On August 13th, the provincial administrator had the children arrested on their way to the fields. At first he tried to get the children to confess that they had made the story up, but he was soon convinced that they were telling the truth. He then tried to persuade them to disclose the secrets the vision had revealed and threatened them with boiling oil when they refused. In fact, so steadfast were the children, that that even though he had them separated and told each one that the others had been boiled to death, not one of them would confess.

October 13th was the date of the last apparition and by then crowds of up to 70,000 people had gathered, among them journalists and photographers. The children had announced that on that day the vision had promised a miracle, "so that all may believe."

As the crowds waited, the mood of anticipation reached 'fever-pitch' and the heavens opened and the most torrential rainstorm thundered down from the sky. In what has come to be known as the "Miracle of the Sun", the heavy rain-clouds parted to reveal a sun that seemed to spin in the sky, sending off radiating spokes of iridescent light, that shimmered and pulsated. Then it appeared to detach itself from the sky and float down to the earth, zigzagging from side to side. After the sun had returned to its proper place, the onlookers examined their clothing and found that, while they had been soaked to the skin a few minutes before, they were now bone-dry.

One journalist described how "the sun, at one moment surrounded with scarlet flame, at another with yellow and deep purple, seemed to move exceedingly fast, at times appearing to be loosened from the sky and to be approaching the earth, strongly radiating heat."

The reporter for the Lisbon daily "O Dia" wrote:

"The silver sun, enveloped in the same gauzy grey light, was seen to whirl and turn in the circle of broken clouds. The light turned a beautiful blue, as if it had come through the stained-glass windows of a cathedral, and spread itself over the people who knelt with outstretched hands. People wept and prayed with uncovered heads, in the presence of a miracle they had awaited. The seconds seemed like hours, so vivid were they."

"As if like a bolt from the blue, the clouds were wrenched apart," said Dr. Formigao, priest and professor at the seminary at Santarem, "and the sun at its zenith appeared in all its splendor. It began to revolve vertiginously on its axis, like the most magnificent firewheel imaginable, taking on all the colors of the rainbow and sending forth multicolored flashes of light, producing the most astounding effect. This sublime and incomparable spectacle, which was repeated three distinct times, lasted for about ten minutes. The immense multitude, overcome by the evidence of such a tremendous prodigy, threw themselves on their knees."

There have been various attempts to give a rational explanation of the "Miracle of the Sun." However, the incident was isolated within a radius of forty miles from the fields near Fatima and no astronomical records exist to confirm unusual solar activity for that date.

Mass hallucination could explain the phenomena, and the appearance of bright lights is not uncommon at large

A Sundog

religious gatherings where the atmosphere reaches a fever pitch of expectation. There are also many close parallels with instances of UFO sightings. However, on this occasion, the crowds weren't exclusively made up of the faithful. There were many atheists, sceptics and journalists present.

Meteorologists have variously explained it as a cloud of stratospheric dust, causing the change in color and softening the solar glare. It may also have been a "sun dog" or parhelion. This "mock sun" is caused by the reflection of sunlight from the particles of ice crystals contained in cirrus clouds. Although this would not explain the "sun dance", such zigzagging movement could be caused by temporary retinal distortion from staring at the bright glare for too long.

Significantly many Protestant evangelicals support a supernatural explanation but see Satan and not the Virgin Mary as the cause.

However the events of that day, no matter how spectacular, have since been overshadowed by the controversy surrounding the three revelations imparted by the apparition, variously known as the Fatima Code or the Secrets of Fatima.

At the second appearance in June 1917, the Virgin had made a prediction that Francisco and Jacinta would die young. Upon being asked by Lucia if they would all go to Heaven, she had replied:

"Yes, I shall take Jacinta and Francisco soon, but you will remain a little longer, since Jesus wishes you to make me known and loved on earth. He wishes also for you to establish devotion in the world to my Immaculate Heart."

Two years later in the Great Spanish Flu Epidemic of 1919, the two children died. Lucia saw further visions in 1925 at the Dorothean convent in Galicia. The first apparition was of the Virgin Mary and the second of the Christ Child. On both occasions, she was asked to convey to the faithful the message of the First Saturday Devotions.

A little while later, Lucia was transferred to another convent where the Virgin reappeared, urging her to reiterate the need for the Consecration of Russia. In 1931, she claimed to have been visited by Jesus, who taught her a new way to pray and entrusted her with a message for the Church episcopacy.

She lived to the ripe old age of 97, spending the second half of her life in a Carmelite convent in Coimbra, Portugal and at her death in 2005, Cardinal Joseph Ratzinger, head of the Congregation for the Doctrine of Faith, issued orders

Medieval illustration of Hell

that her room be sealed off. This gave rise to speculation that there were other messages, which the Church did not want to be made public.

According to Lucia's later account, written in 1942, the first secret predicted the end of World War I and showed her a vision of Hell, which she describes thus:

"Our Lady showed us a great sea of fire which seemed to be under the earth. Plunged in this fire were demons and souls in human form, like transparent burning embers, all blackened or burnished bronze, floating about in the conflagration, now raised into the air by the flames that issued from within themselves together with great clouds of smoke, now falling back on every side like sparks in a huge fire, without weight or equilibrium, and amid shrieks and groans of pain and despair, which horrified us and made us tremble with fear. The demons could be distinguished by their terrifying and repulsive likeness to frightful and unknown animals, all black and transparent. This vision lasted but an instant. How can we ever be grateful enough to our kind heavenly Mother, who had already prepared us by promising, in the first Apparition, to take us to heaven. Otherwise, I think we would have died of fear and terror."

The second secret predicted another war if the faithful neglected their prayers to the Virgin Mary. It also related how sinners could save themselves from the prospect of eternity in Hell:

"You have seen hell where the souls of poor sinners go. To save them, God wishes to establish in the world devotion to my Immaculate Heart. If what I say to you is done, many souls will be saved and there will be peace. The war is going to end: but if people do not cease offending God, a worse one will break out during the Pontificate of Pius XI. When you see a night illumined by an unknown light, know that this is the great sign given you by God that he is about to punish the world for its crimes, by means of war, famine, and persecutions of the Church and of the Holy Father. To prevent this, I shall come to ask for the consecration of Russia to my Immaculate Heart, and the Communion of reparation on the First Saturdays. If my requests are heeded, Russia will be converted, and there will be peace; if not, she will spread her errors throughout

Immaculate Heart of Mary

time of the canonization of her cousins. But the third was sealed in an envelope and entrusted to the Vatican on the agreement that it would not be opened until May 13th 1960, when according to Lucia "it would be more clearly understood."

On that day Pope John XXIII opened and read it and was so shocked at the contents that he refused to publish it, hiding it away in the Vatican archives. Rumors spread that it was the predicted date of the end of the world in a nuclear apocalypse.

And then on May 13th, 1981, on the Feast Day of Our Lady of Fatima, indeed at the very same hour that the vision had appeared to the children, Pope John Paul II was being driven through the crowds in Saint Peter's Square when a Turkish hitman opened fire with a semi-automatic pistol. One of the bullets ripped through the Pope's abdomen, and as he later recalled, he kept himself from slipping into unconsciousness while being rushed to hospital, by focussing his mind on the Virgin Mary.

Our Lady of Fatima

the world, causing wars and persecutions of the Church. The good will be martyred; the Holy Father will have much to suffer; various nations will be annihilated. In the end, my Immaculate Heart will triumph. The Holy Father will consecrate Russia to me, and she shall be converted, and a period of peace will be granted to the world."

The first two secrets were revealed by Lucia at the

It was only later when he was recuperating, that he remembered the significance of the time and date of the attempt on his life. By now the third

Fatima secret had been largely forgotten but he asked that it be brought to him from the archive and must have been

Fatima Shrine grounds

just as shocked as his predecessor to see that it contained a prophecy about a Pope shot by atheists.

This seemed to confirm his conviction that the Virgin Mary had already intervened several times in the course of human history. And so the next year, after a full recovery, he made a pilgrimage to the shrine of the Virgin of Fatima and placed the bullet and his first cardinal ring in the crown of the statue.

"One hand guided the gun," he said, "but another motherly hand guided the bullet millimeters away from vital blood vessels." This had "halted him at the threshold of death."

He also became convinced that he had been saved by the Virgin Mary to fulfil the message concerning the consecration of Russia, for the children's vision seemed to imply that if Russia were consecrated to the Immaculate Heart it would herald an era of world peace.

The rumors that abounded of the involvement of the Kremlin in his assassination and the activity of the Soviets in his homeland Poland led him to identify the Communists with the enemies of the Church.

The man who fired the bullet was Ali Agca who had escaped from prison in Istanbul and found his way to Sofia, the capital of Bulgaria. Travelling in Europe for several weeks, he arrived in Rome in December 1980 and seems to have spent the intervening time making preparations for the assassination in the summer of the following year. Although the theory is still controversial, it was widely believed that he was hired by Bulgarian Soviets

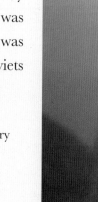

Mother Mary

acting on the orders of the KGB chief Yuri Andropov, who had in turn been instructed by the President of the Soviet Union himself, Leonid Brezhnev.

The Pope's subsequent blessing over all the world, including Russia, given in 1984 is believed by many to have been an attempt to fulfil the Virgin's admonition and the eventual collapse of Communism has come to be seen in many Catholic circles as the fulfilment of the prophecy.

However, the third revelation was still a secret and calls to have it made public intensified, but the Vatican would not alter its stance. During Ali Agca's trial he became obsessed with it and repeatedly requested the publication of the message, perhaps in a deluded attempt to portray his actions as being forced upon him by the hand of fate.

Just a year before the assassination attempt the Pope had told a group of German Catholics:

"If you read that the oceans will inundate continents, and millions of people will die suddenly in a few minutes, once this is known, then in reality it is not necessary to insist on the publication of this Secret."

A report of this meeting appeared in the October 1981 issue of the German Catholic magazine "Stimme des Glaubens" a few months after the assassination attempt, in which the Pope summarized the revelation as a message that prayer, in particular the recitation of the Rosary, is the most effective weapon against evil.

Cardinal Ratzinger's response sounded the same refrain when interviewed in the Pauline Catholic magazine "Jesus" in November 1984: "In the judgement of previous Popes, it adds nothing to what Christians must know respecting that which is stated in the Book of Revelations."

Later that decade on May 13th 1989, the Pope honored the memory of the two siblings who had died in the epidemic by declaring "venerable" Francisco and Jacinta. Eleven years later on the same date, he returned to Fatima to pronounce them "blessed", which is the last step prior to canonization.

It was at this later visit that he announced through his cardinal secretary of state Angelo Sodano that he would finally publicize the third secret.

This served to intensify speculation in the media. The most popular theory was that it alluded to the "End Days", which were almost upon the world. There was even a belief that the message referred to the replacement of the Pope by an imposter, who became identified with the antichrist.

Rosary

Lucia's silence on the matter led to the rumor that she had been forbidden to speak of it by the Vatican, although her austere life of silence and seclusion as a Carmelite nun would have made such an injunction largely unnecessary. She repeatedly described herself as a very private person and at the time of the apparitions she had actually wanted to keep them secret but was prevented from doing so by her cousin Jacinta, who was an inveterate chatterbox.

However, she had hinted at what was contained in the third secret. When interviewed in a catholic journal about the articles that were appearing in newspapers around the world, she urged the readers to study chapters 8 through to 13 of the Book of Revelations.

When the secret was finally released, people were left rather unsatisfied. The controversy seems to stem from the Vatican's insistence on withholding it until nearly twenty years after the assassination attempt. If it referred only to this, what possible reason could there be for keeping it secret for such a long time after the event?

There were also those who claimed that it had been tampered with, a part of the message withheld. In her fourth memoir, Lucia had hinted that the third secret began with the words, "In Portugal, the dogma of the faith will always be preserved…" The fact that these words did not appear led to accusations of a cover-up.

The most plausible reason for the delay, which went against the specific instructions of Lucia, seemed to be that the message contained unfavorable remarks about the Pope, hence leading him to withhold it from the public. When no such remarks were forthcoming, the conspiracy theorists had a field day.

The text also seemed more ambiguous than the last two secrets, which contained specific information. This added to the conviction that people had been fobbed off.

According to Cardinal Tarcisio Bertone in his Companion document from the "Congregation for the Doctrine of Faith," the release of the third secret supposedly "marks the end of the age of lust for power and evil." However as the September 11 terrorist attacks occurred only one year after the announcement of the message, it can hardly be claimed to have ushered in an era of world peace.

Defenders of the prophecy would argue that the promise of peace was dependent on the consecration of Russia and as Russia was not named in the blessing of 1984, the Virgin's instructions had not been fulfilled. They also

The 9/11 attacks on the Twin Towers

argue that Sister Lucia did not claim that the secret would bring world peace, only that the world would then be ready to understand the import of the message.

However, the anti-Communist nature of the visions has inspired a society called the Blue Army of our Lady, who believe that they are fulfilling the promise of the message by dedicating themselves to daily prayer and the devotion of the Rosary and in this way they are preparing the way for the peace that was predicted after the collapse of Communism.

Lucia's words, written shortly before the date of the 1960 release of the message, indicate that it concerns the increasing secularization of the world:

"Father, the devil is in the mood for engaging in a decisive battle against the Blessed Virgin. And the devil knows what it is that most offends God and will gain for him the greatest number of souls. Thus, the devil does everything to overcome souls consecrated to God, because in this way the devil will succeed in leaving souls of the faithful abandoned by their leaders, thereby the more easily will he seize them."

This chimes in with the statement made by Mario Cardinal Ciappi, papal theologian under Pope John Paul II that: "In the third secret it is foretold, among other things, that the great apostasy in the Church will begin at the top."

In 1984 Cardinal Ratzinger (the present Pope Benedict XVI) linked the third secret to "the dangers threatening the faith and the life of the Christian, and therefore of the world. And then the importance of the 'novissimi' (the last events at the end of time)."

The Bishop of Fatima, Cosme do Amaral's position was rather different: "Its content concerns only our faith. To identify the [third] secret with catastrophic announcements or with a nuclear holocaust is to deform the meaning of the message. The loss of faith of a continent is worse than the annihilation of a nation; and it is true that faith is continually diminishing in Europe."

Pope John Paul II admitted in 1980, a year before the attempt on his life, that his predecessors had not yet released the secret "so as not to encourage the world power of Communism to make certain moves."

Disapproving of those who sought to know the message from a sensation-seeking curiosity he reiterated the call for the use of the Rosary:

"Here is the remedy against this evil. Pray, pray, and ask for nothing more. Leave everything else to the Mother of God."

Some people have argued that the Fatima prophecies were exploited by the Church, which in effect made something out of next to nothing, seizing on the questionable experiences of three impressionable young children and turning it into a cult. This was after all an era when the Church felt it was under siege from the forces of modernism. The Republican revolution of 1910 had seen the Church's influence in society on the wane. The Church became increasingly paranoid that it was being persecuted by a sinister mixture of Freemasonry and godless Communism.

The political situation was polarized between the urban liberals and the conservative rural Catholics. The fact that the children were arrested in an effort to prevent a recurrence of the visions indicates the potential that these visions had of unifying and inspiring the masses.

Following the military coup in 1928 and the resurgence of the counter-revolutionaries, in much the same way that Catholicism was wedded to nationalism in

Virgin Mary

Spain under Franco, belief in the Fatima prophecies was encouraged as a form of patriotic pride in Portugal.

Whether you are a believer or not, there is no denying the power of the vision:

"After the two parts which I have already explained, at the left of Our Lady and a little above, we saw an angel with a flaming sword in his left hand; flashing, it gave out flames that looked as though they would set the world on fire; but they died out in contact with the splendour that Our Lady radiated towards him from her right hand. Pointing to the earth with his right hand, the Angel cried out in a loud voice: "Penance, Penance, Penance!""

"And we saw in an immense light that is God: something similar to how people appear in a mirror when they pass in front of it, a bishop dressed in White. We had the impression that it was the Holy Father.

"Other bishops and priests were going up a steep mountain, at the top of which there was a big Cross of rough-hewn trunks as of a cork-tree with the bark; before reaching there the Holy Father passed through a big city half in ruins and half trembling with halting step, afflicted with pain and sorrow, he prayed for the souls of the corpses he met on his way. Having reached the top of the mountain, on his knees at the foot of the big Cross he was killed by a group of soldiers who fired bullets and arrows at him, and in the same way there died one after another the other bishops, priests and various lay people of different ranks and positions.

"Beneath the two arms of the Cross, there were two Angels each with a crystal aspersorium in his hand, in which they gathered up the blood of the martyrs and with it sprinkled the souls that were making their way to God."

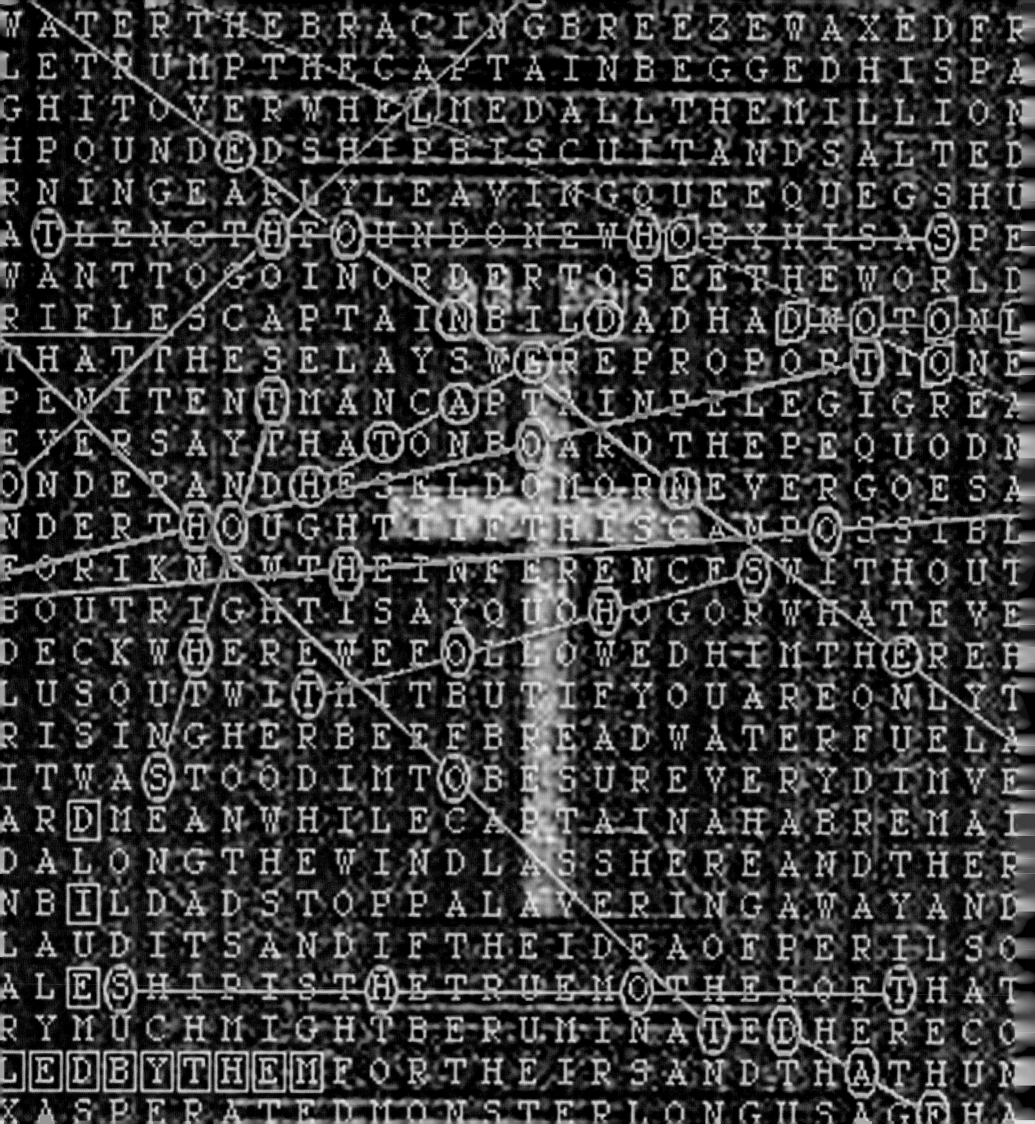

chapter 4

One thing you are not likely to have been told in school about Sir Isaac Newton is that alongside his well-known work on physics and mathematics, he was intensely interested in religion, in particular with the theory that there was a code beyond the written words of the Bible. Indeed, it could well be argued that he devoted more time and energy to this and other alchemical areas of research than all his other more recognizably scientific lines of enquiry put together.

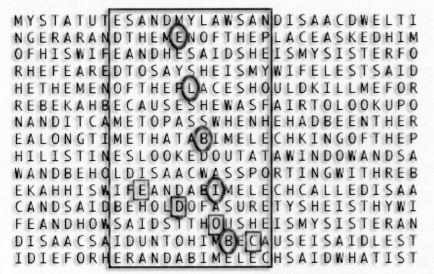

```
MYSTATUTESANDMYLAWSANDISAACDWELTI
NGERARANDTHEMENOFTHEPLACEASKEDHIM
OFHISWIFEANDHESAIDSHEISMYSISTERFO
RHEFEAREDTOSAYSHEISMYWIFELESTSAID
HETHEMENOFTHEPLACESHOULDKILLMEFOR
REBEKAHBECAUSESHEWASFAIRTOLOOKUPO
NANDITCAMETOPASSWHENHEHADBEENTHER
EALONGTIMETHATABIMELECHKINGOFTHEP
HILISTINESLOOKEDOUTATAWINDOWANDSA
WANDBEHOLDISAACWASSPORTINGWITHREB
EKAHHISWIFEANDABIMELECHCALLEDISAA
CANDSAIDBEHOLDOFASURETYSHEISTHYWI
FEANDHOWSAIDSTTHOUSHEISMYSISTERAN
DISAACSAIDUNTOHIMBECAUSEISAIDLEST
IDIEFORHERANDABIMELECHSAIDWHATIST
```

The Bible

The full extent of his work can only be guessed at because shortly before his death, he gathered several of his closest friends to help him burn a great number of boxes containing manuscripts and personal journals, although "Observations upon the Prophecies of Daniel and the Apocalypse of Saint John" is still extant.

Newton believed that the bible was a "cryptogram set by the Almighty" and he wrote over a million words describing his quest to "read the riddle of the Godhead, the riddle of the past and future events divinely fore-ordained."

However, despite his phenomenal intelligence, he was ultimately to fail in his quest to penetrate beyond the veil and he went to his deathbed without the answers he was so desperately seeking.

However, towards the end of the second millennium AD two men seemed to have made the discovery that so eluded Newton. They seemed finally to have broken the Bible code.

Before we look at the work of Israeli mathematician Eliyahu Rips and American reporter Michael Drosnin, we have to go back in time to the first half of the twentieth century when Rabbi Weissmadel was studying the Torah (the first five

Isaac Newton

books of the Old Testament) in Prague. He discovered that if he skipped fifty letters from the beginning of Genesis and kept skipping the same distance the letters spelled out the word "Torah." He tried this in the books Exodus, Numbers and Deuteronomy and the same word appeared.

Professor Rips heard about this discovery in the early eighties and repeated the experiment. His mathematical background enabled him to make more advanced studies than the simple method of sequential counting undertaken by Weissman. And when he teamed up with physicist Doron Witzum, the mathematical model they arrived at with the

Torah Scroll

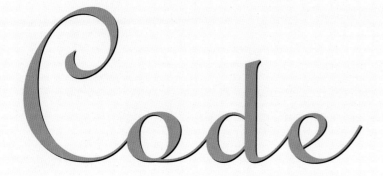

benefits of sophisticated computer programs resulted in some astounding discoveries.

The bulk of the research was done at Jerusalem College of technology and a paper was ready to be published in the scholarly journal Statistical Science, a peer review journal of the Institute of Mathematical Studies in August 1994. The editor was moved to write an introduction to the article in which he stated:

"Our referees were baffled; their prior beliefs made them think the Book of Genesis could not possibly contain meaningful references to modern-day individuals, yet when the authors carried out additional analyses and checks, the effect persisted."

Investigating the phenomenon of Equidistant Letter Sequences, the authors took the names and birth-dates of thirty-two personalities from the Enyclopaedia of Great Men of Israel, and looked to see whether they were encoded in four pieces of text: two early writings in Hebrew, the initial segment of Tolstoy's War and Peace and the Book of Genesis. Only in the latter were the names encoded. Then they took the names and dates and jumbled them up into ten million combinations and ran them through the computer program to see whether these new random pairings came together in the Book of Genesis. But none of them did.

The news that there was statistically meaningful information encoded into the first five books of the Bible about people born after the Pentateuch was written shook the world, let alone the scientific community. One of the top code-breakers at the U.S. National Security Agency, Harold Glans was positive the experiment had to be flawed and set out to disprove it by writing his own computer program and checking to see whether he could replicate the results. He also decided to check for the cities in which these thirty-two people were born and when, much to his surprise, he found the information he was looking for, he became a firm believer in the code's authenticity.

Rips's genius was to run the whole of the Torah together with no spaces between the words so that it appears as one long stream of 304,805 letters, which, according to Jewish legends, was the way Moses received it from God in an act of divine amanuensis. The computer program then searches for a key word by beginning at the first letter and performing a skip sequence of one to many thousands, working its way through to the end and then starting again from the second letter and so on. The program then arranges the text in rows of however many letters were contained in the skip sequence. Thus, the Torah becomes a living ever-changing entity, which contains an infinite amount of possible permutations. Each search term is like a key, which opens up new matrices of information and related words appear to gather round

the keyword, criss-crossing diagonally, horizontally, some even in geometric shapes.

If indeed the Torah were one long string of letters, constituting in effect a complex computer program, this would explain the Jewish tradition that if so much as one letter was copied down wrong, it could not be used and must indeed be buried.

Time and time again, important events in the history, not just of the Israelites, but of mankind as a whole, seem to be encoded in the Bible many years before they happened. The date Neil Armstrong landed on the moon appears next to "Man on moon", "spaceship" and even "Apollo 11." The words "Watergate", "Nixon" and the date 1974, when he resigned all appear together, with the phrase "Who is he? President, but he was kicked out." A search for "Hitler" turned up "evil man", "Nazi and enemy" and "slaughter." "Eichmann" was encoded with "Zyklon B" the gas used in the concentration camps.

A professor of mathematics at Yale University, I. Piatetski-Shapiro, was so moved by the results he declared,

"There is no way within the known laws of mathematics to explain seeing the future. Newtonian physics is too simple to explain a set of predictions this complex and detailed. Quantum physics is also not enough. What we're talking about here is some intelligence that stands outside."

It seemed that Newton was right to look for a code within the text of the Bible but despite his brilliant mind, he was not equipped with a tool that was up to the job. Mankind would have to wait over three hundred years for the progress in computer science to unlock the code.

Indeed, in the text where God speaks to Moses, telling him, "Behold I make a covenant: before all thy people I will work miracles", encoded behind the text is the

A charcoal drawing of Moses

World War

Atomic explosion over Nagasaki

apocalyptic warnings that crop up in the hidden code.

Drosnin and Rips searched the code for any number matches with the words "World War" and "Atomic Holocaust." They had already found "Hiroshima" with a skip sequence of 1945, the year that the first atom bomb was dropped. These words came together twice, once with the number 2000 and again with 2006. Coincidentally, this occurred at a place in the bible that is considered so sacred that practising Jews in Israel keep it in a separate scroll fastened to the doorway of their homes. This part of the bible, 170 words long, is known as the Mezuzah and God has explicit instructions on how they must be treated:

"And these words, which I command thee this day, shall be in thy heart; and thou shalt teach them diligently to thy children, and shalt talk of them when thou sittest in thy house, and when thou walkest by the way, and when thou liest down, and when thou risest up. And thou shalt bind them for a sign upon thy arm, and between thy eyes. And thou shalt write them upon thy gates."

Was the purpose of this strict admonishment to ensure that should the written words of the Bible somehow be destroyed, this crucial piece of the code would be preserved

word "computer" and it appears again in Exodus, in the description of the Ark, built to house the stone tablets on which are engraved the Ten Commandments: "It was made by computer."

Michael Drosnin postulates that as the root of the Hebrew word for "computer" is the same for "thought", what is meant by "computer" may well be "mind", the mind of God.

Two verses in the Book of Daniel and the Book of Revelations immediately present themselves as of the utmost significance. Coincidentally, each contains the most apocalyptic visions found anywhere in the bible. Daniel is visited by an angel and the future is revealed to him but then he is told to "shut up the words, and seal the book until the time of the End." In Revelations we hear of a secret book "written within and on the backside, sealed with seven seals. And no man in Heaven nor in Earth, neither under the earth, was able to open the book, neither to look thereon."

Was it possible that when the angel told Daniel that "the words are closed up and sealed 'til the time of the End", he meant a code that would only be revealed when man reached a certain stage of technological advancement? And if so, does this mean that the End of Days is upon us? It certainly does seem to coincide with a plethora of

and handed down by word of mouth, so that one day, its warning of impending Armageddon could be heeded?

With the collapse of the Soviet Union in the early nineties, it looked as though the threat of nuclear war, which had hung over the world ever since Hiroshima, had finally faded away. It seemed for a while there was no one left to fight. But the Bible code revealed the new threat the world was facing with chilling accuracy. One word says it all and it appeared right next to "atomic holocaust" and "World War": "Terrorism."

We are now faced with the terrifying predicament of a former super power, which seems to lack both the will and the resources to properly secure its nuclear arsenal and cannot afford to pay its extremely well-educated and disaffected nuclear physicists. Never before have such awesome weapons of mass destruction come so close to the reach of groups or even individuals with the will to use them for their own ends. Hitherto, it has been the preserve of James Bond movies.

The principle of Mutual Assured Destruction had always seemed to ensure that nuclear missiles would only ever act as a deterrent, never as a weapon of aggression. But now we are faced with a global situation where groups of religious fanatics actively welcome their own destruction, so long as they can take enough of the infidels with them.

In the light of this possibility, several apocalyptic verses in the bible seemed to be chillingly accurate descriptions of the aftermath of a nuclear attack, all the more impressive as they were written by a culture whose most advanced ballistic weaponry was the bow and arrow. One verse in particular makes the skin prickle,

"Brought low, you will speak from the ground, your speech will mumble out of the dust, your voice will come ghostlike from the earth, out of the dust you will whisper. And your many enemies will become like fine dust, the ruthless hordes like blown chaff. It will happen suddenly, in an instant."

More chilling still is the appearance adjacent to "atomic weapon" and "World War" of "Jerusalem", which is widely acknowledged to be the potential flashpoint for an explosion of violence between the Jews and the Arabs which could engulf the rest of the world in a global conflict that would make World War II look like a playground fight.

The Book of Ezekiel warns that the threat to Israel

World War II
Red Army Soldiers

Destruction caused in Tangshan, China due to the Great Earthquake in 1976

is from the north: "You will come from your place in the far north, you and many nations with you, a great horde, a mighty army."

This would seem to indicate an attack by Syria and indeed Syria is encoded in the selfsame verse, with two allied nations: Persia and Phut, which are respectively modern-day Iran and Libya.

Accompanying the apocalyptic vision of Total War in Ezekiel, Isaiah and Revelations are predictions of earthquakes wreaking devastation on an unprecedented scale, such as:

"I will make the heavens tremble, and the Earth will shake from its place. Men will flee to caves in the rocks and to holes in the ground from dread of the Lord when he rises to shake the Earth."

The Bible code revealed similar warnings to Drosnin and Rips for quakes in 2014 and 2113 accompanied by the words "Desolated, Empty, Depopulated" and "For Everyone, the Great Terror: Fire, Earthquake."

And given the correct encoding of the dates of the San Franciso earthquakes with the words "S.F. Calif" and the juxtaposition of the year 1976, China and "Great Earthquake" in which 800,000 people died, it would appear that we ignore these warnings at our peril.

But an event of even more cataclysmic proportions is to be found within the bible for those who have managed to "open the sealed book." Just as the asteroid that hit the earth 65 million years ago, wiping out the dinosaurs, is hidden in the code, there is a warning of another comet that may strike the earth in 2126. Next to the date when the comet was first spotted, September 27 1992, which was the Hebrew New Year were the words "Eve of New Year, Swift", Swift-Tuttle being the name given to the comet.

Just in case anyone was in doubt about the accuracy of the prediction, in July 1994 a comet called "Shoemaker-Levy" crashed into the planet Jupiter. Two months before the collision, Drosnin correctly predicted it from the code, in fact the information was so accurate and complete it could have been used as a media wire report after the event.

Later that same year, Drosnin found in the code the name of the then Israeli Prime Minister Yitzak Rabin crossed by the words "assassin that will assassinate."

He took the warning to a close friend of Rabin's, the poet Chaim Guri, who passed it on, but nothing was done. A year later, Rabin was indeed dead, shot in the back by a gunman called Amir whose name appeared right above Rabin's, along with the time and place. Unfortunately these exact details only revealed themselves after the event when Drosnin knew what to look for.

The next Prime Minister Shimon Peres took Drosnin more seriously and invited the reporter to meet with him in Jerusalem. Drosnin showed him the juxtaposition of related words that cropped up when the search term "Holocaust of Israel" was fed into the computer program: "Atomic Artilleryman" "Libya" and "The Pisgah" which is a mountain range in Jordan, where the Bible seemed to warn a nuclear weapon could be concealed.

However, in the same location were the words "In order that you prolong your days" which seemed to indicate that the future was not set in stone, and the holocaust could be averted.

The series of suicide bombings in early 1996 that effectively ended the tentative peace between Israel and Palestine seemed to confirm the prediction that Total War was on the horizon. Once again, they were successfully picked up by Drosnin and Rips.

When Benjamin Netenyahu was elected Prime Minister, Drosnin began to find phrases that eerily echoed those predicting Rabin's murder: "Surely he will be killed", "his soul was cut off."

But then, something peculiar happened. Firstly Drosnin found the words "July to Amman" next to the prediction of Netenyahu's murder and not long afterwards the Prime Minister's trip was confirmed in the newspapers. But then Netenyahu fell ill and the trip was cancelled.

Was this the first instance of the bible code getting it wrong, he wondered? But then Rips pointed out the word "delayed" above his name. The date for the murder and the ensuing atomic holocaust came and went. Had it been averted because of the cancellation? Might World War I have been averted if the Archduke Ferdinand had not been in the wrong place at the wrong time and hence avoided the assassin's bullet?

Drosnin now began to find questions in the code such as "will you change it?" as though the code was a living intelligent entity that was reacting to world events and indeed to Drosnin's research. Next to the word "delayed" he found "Five futures, five roads." Were there in fact many different possible futures, all the ramifications of the potential combinations of events? Could the Bible Code foresee them

NASA image of Comet Shoemaker-Levy 9 taken by the Hubble Space Telescope

The Torah Scroll

all and help us to choose the right path? Was this in fact a way of reconciling the apparently incompatible phenomena of Free Will and Pre-ordination? And so was the mind of God rather like a Chess Grandmaster that could see the outcomes of every move his opponent could make but did not thereby remove his power to choose?

These are questions that are still being asked. The Bible Code has been refuted by a prominent mathematician who got the same results as Drosnin from a copy of "Moby Dick", despite Rips' claim that he rigorously tested his hypothesis on a copy of "Crime and Punishment" and "War and Peace."

2006 came up repeatedly for the End of Days, with a comet, a world-shaking earthquake and an atomic holocaust. Chances are, if you're still around to read this, the code got it wrong, and a code that can't get it right is no code at all.

chapter 5

In June 1099, after a gruelling journey in which they had been beset every step of the way, not only by enemy ambush, but by the extremes of weather and the privations of an army on the march, the crusaders finally arrived before the walls of Jerusalem and found that their troubles were only just beginning.

Betrayal of

The wells outside the city had been poisoned on the orders of the Egyptian governor, and the peasant flocks driven away. There was no shade from the searing heat of the sun and this was not just insufferable for men in full battle dress, it also meant there was no local timber to build the machines of war necessary to take a walled city.

There were already plenty of Christians living in Jerusalem, who were well tolerated by the Moslems, but the governor thought that by expelling them he would transfer the burden of feeding them onto the Crusaders.

As it turned out, this was a fatal error, for among them was a man named Gerard, master of the Amalfi hostelry for Christian pilgrims, and he had a great deal

of information to share on the weak points of the city's fortifications.

Jerusalem fell after a siege that lasted nine days, and there followed scenes of the most shameful carnage as the triumphant invaders inflicted a frenzied vengeance on the enemy that is graphically summed up in a report sent to the Pope:

"If you would hear how we treated our enemies in Jerusalem, know that in the portico of Solomon and in the Temple, our men rode through the unclean blood of the Saracens, which came up to the knees of their horses."

Knight Templar

Saint John of Jerusalem

For their part in the victory, the monks who ran the Amalfi hostelry were given grants of land and gifts of treasure, and with Jerusalem opened up, they grew into a large and thriving order. In 1118, they decided to expand their operation to include knights who would devote themselves to protecting the Christian pilgrims, pouring in from all over Europe. They changed their name to the Hospital of Saint John of Jerusalem and would ever after be known as the Hospitallers.

Prompted no doubt by the success of this order, Hugh de Payans, a vassal of the Count of Champagne, petitioned King Baldwin II for royal sanction of an order

he intended to establish with eight other knights. Pledging themselves to a life of poverty, chastity and obedience, the raison d'etre of the Templars would be the protection of pilgrims.

Little is known of the actions of the new order over the next nine years, except that it seems they took in no new members and were quartered in a wing of the royal palace, the former al—Aqsa mosque, which stood on the site of the Temple of Solomon.

Al—Aqsa mosque

Then in 1127, Pope Honarius was petitioned on behalf of the Templars by the abbot of Clairvaux, Saint Bernard, who was a man of such prestige in the Church that he was known as the "second Pope".

A council was convened at Troyes where the order was granted official papal recognition and a Rule was established, governing their daily lives and activities.

The council of Troyes marked a changing point in the fortunes of the order. With papal sanction, the Templars transcended all sovereign authority and were answerable only to the Pope. Laying down their lives in the defense of Christians making the pilgrimage to the Holy Land was seen as such a worthy and honorable cause that gifts and new recruits flooded in, especially from Europe's noble families. Service in the Templars was said to be sufficient penance to expiate the guilt of any crime, even the worst of all, heresy. This was to prove significant in the years to come when the Church would seek to suppress the order, on the grounds of desecrating the cross and the holy sacrament.

It is quite probable that during the Albigensian crusade, when the Cathar heretics in southern France were massacred, a number

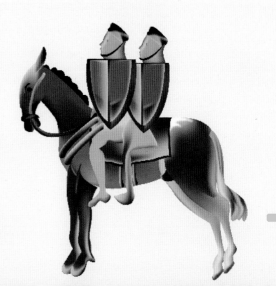

of the high-ranking Cathar nobles may have joined the order. No doubt, the presence of such freethinkers would have opened the Templar minds to the various Gnostic and Dualist heresies that had gone underground to escape persecution by the Church.

The order grew rich very rapidly. For a start, the vow of poverty precluded the ownership of property, which meant everything, from castles and land, right down to the smallest of pocket books, had to be donated to the order upon entry as was any loot taken in battle. Money was further saved by the rule that if a Templar knight was captured on the field, he could not be ransomed. However, it usually never got to this stage, as the knights could not retreat unless the odds against them were at least three-to-one. Even in the face of overwhelming odds, a commander might order his men to fight to the death and they would have to obey.

Over the next two centuries, some 20,000 initiates were to join the order, the vast majority of them from the nobility. Second-born sons might bring a dowry of money with them, first-borns their entire inheritance.

It was reckoned at the time that the Templars owned over nine thousand revenue-producing manors, as well as mills and markets. Add to this the donations from the Church in Rome and revenue earned from transporting pilgrims to the Holy Land in Templar-owned ships, and it will be appreciated what an immensely wealthy order the Templars were.

As servants of God who had pledged themselves to an extremely austere and dangerous life, the Templars were viewed as one of the most trustworthy institutions in Europe. They already had the means and the manpower to guard their immense fortune, it was not long before noble families across Europe realized that here was one of the most reliable safe deposits for their wealth when they travelled abroad.

Knight Templar riding

In fact, so secure were their vaults and such trust placed in their honesty that for a while the crown jewels of the English royal family were placed with them.

They soon expanded from safety deposits to the issuing of paper for money, maintaining trusts for noble scions and even a precursor of mortgage banking. The issuance of paper money is something we take for granted nowadays, but it would have been incredibly useful to someone wanting to transfer funds overseas. The only alternative available at the time was to physically transport the gold and silver there yourself, which was a risky venture.

If the system is to escape outside exploitation, it requires a very effective network of communication, with means of verifying identification. With the military network that was already in place, this would not have proved too big a step. From their dealings with the Saracens, the Templars were well-versed in the cut-and-thrust of espionage and counter-espionage, and the practice of using codes to conceal operations intelligence was already highly evolved.

Secret agents, many of them Moslems, were on the Templar payroll in cities all along the coast of the Mediterranean in both continents. Their influence extended even to Cairo, where they employed the Emir al-Fakhri as a double agent.

The necessarily clandestine nature of much of the Templar activity added to the air of mystery that shrouded

the organization. But it was not just those on the outside looking in who were kept in the dark, the atmosphere of secrecy pervaded the internal infrastructure of the order.

There were three classes: the knights, the sergeants and the clerics.

Those in the knightly class were designated full brothers and they were required not only to be "free", that is to say not born as a bondsman or serf, but also to derive from the nobility. They wore a white mantle with a red eight-pointed cross and a sheepskin girdle which symbolized their oath of chastity. They wore their hair very short but did not cut their beards. The sergeants were recruited from the free bourgeoisie. They wore a black mantle with a red cross and performed the duties of squires and sentries.

The clerics attended to the pastoral care of the Templars, serving mass and hearing confession. They dressed in a green mantle with a red cross and always wore gloves to keep their hands clean for "when they touched God" in the performance of the holy sacrament. Because the knights were illiterate, they also acted as scribes. In contrast to the knights, they were clean-shaven.

Right at the top of the order was the Grandmaster, who ruled with absolute authority. His headquarters were in Jerusalem and as well as holding the position of abbot he was a full-equipped and trained knight, who expected to die on the battlefield. Of twenty-one Grandmasters in total, ten died in action.

Strict secrecy was observed between the classes and between the different ranks within each class. Knowledge of the Rule would be gradually revealed as an initiate rose through the ranks. Only those at the very top of the hierarchy would be in full possession of the Templar secrets. Such importance was placed on hermetically sealing each rung of the order, that meetings could only take place with guards outside with drawn swords and any breach of the oath of secrecy resulted in expulsion from the order and in some cases even death.

Thus the Templars' reputation for secrecy was well-deserved and when the order was brutally suppressed in 1307, it played a crucial role in the fate of those who managed to survive the initial wave of persecution.

The fortunes of the Christian powers in the Holy Land waxed and waned in the two centuries following the formation of the Templars but in 1291, the last Christian stronghold at Acre fell to the Mamelukes, and with it went a significant portion of the Templar wealth and possessions.

They set up base on the island of Cyprus, but ran into trouble because of the threat such a well-equipped and well-trained standing army posed to the sovereign, King Henry. Compounding this issue for an order, which recognized no authority save the Pope, was the problem of what to do now that their whole raison d'etre of

King Philip IV of France

providing safe passage to the Holy Land for Christian pilgrims, was redundant.

They were eager for another crusade, but the response from the Church and the ruling families of Europe was not favorable. The Teutonic Knights were attempting to conquer the pagans in north-eastern Europe and the Hospitallers were busy trying to establish a base on Rhodes, which they finally managed in 1308 and from then on were known as the Knights of Rhodes.

In 1306 Pope Clement V called the Grandmaster of the Templars to Poitiers for what he thought would be a discussion about the possibility of a new crusade. Little did he know it then, but the days of the Templars were numbered and powerful men were plotting their downfall and the division of the spoils.

King Philip IV of France had long looked on the Templar wealth with greedy eyes. He had borrowed heavily from the Templar treasury to finance his wars against King Edward I of England. To strike at the Templars would be a double-blow, at once cancelling the debt and plundering their legendary wealth. The one thing that was standing in his way was papal sanction.

To understand the mindset of the papacy, it is necessary to go back a decade or so to the death of Pope Nicholas IV in 1292. At that time, there were two major political forces in Rome, the Colonna and

King Henry VIII

Orsini families, who controlled the cardinals with a shifting but roughly equal sway. As neither faction could agree on a successor, they elected an old man who was not expected to live long and hence would buy time for a decision to be reached.

Pietro Morrone was a member of the Celestine order, whose followers were pledged to poverty and chastity and given to whipping themselves and fasting to drive out sinful thoughts. He would have been wholly unfit for the job, were he in his prime, but he was already showing signs of senility. The change of surroundings from his mountain cave to the opulent but precarious corridors of power left him bewildered and prey to the machinations of the French King of Naples, Charles II. He easily persuaded him to elect thirteen new cardinals, of whom ten owed their allegiance to Charles II, seven being French and three Napolitan.

The cardinals realized too late that they were in grave danger of losing their influence to the vested interests of the French monarchy and they tried to force Celestine V to abdicate. Legend has it that cardinal Benedetto Gaetani stood behind the tapestries in the Pope's chamber at night and whispered to the terrified Pope as he lay in his bed, telling him that he was a messenger from God, and that the Pope had greatly displeased the Almighty and must resign or face the consequences. When Celestine V duly gave up his post, Gaetani aligned himself with the French faction, which now had the casting vote. With the backing of the Orsini family, he was elected Pope Boniface VIII.

However, one consequence of the principle of the divine sanction of the papal seat is that people will not accept that it can be renounced by resignation. By tradition,

Popes have always occupied the Throne of Peter until they passed away. Thus many pilgrims refused to recognize Boniface VIII and made their pilgrimages to Celestine instead. Boniface's response was to have the old man arrested and thrown into a cell so small that he was reputedly unable to lie down properly. Unsurprisingly, in the spring of 1296, he died.

But Boniface's problems did not end there. The Colonna family continued to contest his election, claiming he had unlawfully assumed the papal mantle. Boniface reacted just as robustly, stripping the Colonna cardinals of their benefices and declaring their lands and property forfeit to the Church and barring them from holding holy offices for the next four generations.

In what amounted to a holy war against the family, he offered pardons and indulgences to all who would join in the papal crusade against these new enemies of the Church. Before long, the Colonna had been beaten back to their stronghold in Palestrina where they managed to hold out against the besiegers. When it became obvious that the fortress could not be taken, Boniface arrived and offered a full pardon to the Colonna cardinals sheltering inside should they come to terms, a promise which was duly broken the moment they surrendered.

Flushed with success, Boniface declared that his was the highest authority in the world, deriving as it did from Jesus Christ through Saint Peter. This meant that all temporal or secular rulers were beholden to the Pope, and received their mandate to rule from him. Naturally, many of the royal families of Europe were not very impressed with this claim, in particular King Philip IV of France,

Pope Boniface VIII

who imposed a new tax on Church revenue within his borders. When Boniface protested, Philip imposed a ban on the export of silver and gold from France without his permission, designed to interrupt the flow of money to the Vatican coffers.

Luckily for Boniface, the turn of the century was traditionally a time of religious pilgrimage, and Boniface promised absolution for all crimes for those who made the journey to Rome. Reportedly, so many came bearing gifts for the Church, that at the Church of Saint Paul, pilgrims had to fight their way to the altar, where priests stood with wooden rakes working in shifts to sweep the gold and silver into chests and bags, so fast was it being heaped up.

Boniface became a veritable megalo-maniac, dressing in the insignia of the old Roman Empire, with heralds going before him declaring "Behold! I am Caesar!" bearing two swords, symbolizing his authority over both the spiritual and secular worlds.

When the jubilee celebrations died down, he called the clergy to Rome to discuss the problems with France. Philip responded by calling a council of his own, insisting that the French clergy attend. The French nation, both commoners and nobility, united behind Philip in his claim that he held his throne directly from God, and not through the Pope. The clergy were urged to show their loyalty to Philip by condemning Boniface IV. An impasse was reached, with Philip warning that any cardinal attending a council called to criticize the king would be stripped of his property and privileges, and Boniface threatening any clergy who did not attend with equally severe consequences.

The Pope's response was to issue the papal bull "Unam Sanctam", the controversial edict, which decrees that not only is the Pope the supreme ruler this side of the gates of the kingdom of Heaven, but "it is a condition of salvation that all human beings should be subject to the Pontiff of Rome."

In other words, anyone siding with Philip in his claim to bypass the Pope in the chain of command between Heaven and Earth would be denied eternal bliss in the company of God and his heavenly host of angels.

Philip went on the attack. With the shadowy figure of Guillaume de Nogaret as his agent provocateur, a propaganda campaign was launched against the Pope in which it was claimed that Boniface was guilty of murder, blasphemy, sodomy, heresy, stealing from Church funds, divulging secrets learned in the confessional seal of secrecy, and even of having sex with a pet demon that lived in a jewel set in his ring!

The document had the desired effect of uniting France in condemnation of the Pope and calls for his impeachment rang out across the country, even from the clergy. The anti-Roman sentiment was strengthened by the sympathy the nation felt for their king, who had been personally excommunicated by Boniface.

This was too much for Boniface to bear and he took the unprecedented step of announcing that on September 8th, 1303, he would issue a proclamation placing every single loyal subject of King Philip under ecclesiastical censure. This presented a very serious problem to Philip, for in theory it had the potential to deny French Christians the right to Church burial, absolution for their sins and baptism for their children. It could have provoked the nation into an uprising against their King, and so de Nogaret was entrusted with the mission of preventing the Pope from issuing it at any cost.

Bernard de Goth

Enlisting the help of the Colonna family, which had suffered so much at the hands of Boniface, he took a small army to the town of Anangni, from where the Pope was due to make the announcement, and with the help of local civic leaders, he captured the Pope the night before the proclamation was due to be issued.

Boniface was already 86 years old and by all accounts very roughly handled. Sciarra Colonna was in favor of killing him there and then, but de Nogaret knew that this would greatly harm Philip's cause and wanted to put him on trial. In the event the local townspeople had come to regret their complicity in the Pope's capture and returned in great numbers to drive away the small force.

However, the treatment he had received meant that Boniface was a broken man and he died soon after.

Surprisingly the monarchies of Europe did not wish to make capital out of Philip's involvement in the death of Boniface and within ten days, a new Pope had been elected. Benedict XI, perhaps sensing his vulnerability in the face of such open aggression from France, tried to effect a rapprochement, but Philip took this as a sign of weakness and demanded a posthumous trial of Boniface for the alleged charges. Benedict could not possibly countenance such an attack on the Holy See and reacted by excommunicating all those involved in the "Crime of Anagni." Within a matter of weeks, he too was dead and once again the name of de Nogaret came up with dark mutterings of plots and poison.

A year after his death, the cardinals had still not appointed a successor, so divided were they as to the worth of the several candidates. Philip saw his chance to elect someone who would comply with his designs on the fabled Templar wealth. He came up with the idea that the French faction would stay out of the initial round of voting and would then choose one of three candidates selected by the Orsini and Colonna factions, who had been restored to prominence in the Conclave after Boniface's demise. Knowing full well that the French cardinals were under his sway, he was confident that he could guarantee a Pope favorably disposed towards his plans.

Bernard de Goth, the archbishop of Bordeaux, looked like the most pliable, as his zealous ambition to sit on the Throne of Peter was widely known, and so Philip set about cutting a deal. In return for the official condemnation of Boniface, the removal of the excommunication of Philip,

Benedict XI

and the right to tax the French clergy at ten percent, Bernard de Goth was duly appointed to the position of supreme pontiff. To seal the deal, de Goth or Clement V as he styled himself, swore a binding oath and gave up his brothers and two nephews as hostage to the bargain. It is widely agreed that there was a secret clause to the covenant, never written down, that he would assist Philip in his suppression of the Templar order.

On his way from Bordeaux to Rome, Clement V, with twenty-three new French cardinals in his retinue, settled in Avignon for what was supposed to be only a short stay of rest. However, the French influence was by now so strong that it was decided the papal seat should remain within France and over the next seventy-five years in a period that would henceforth be known as the "Babylonish Captivity", only one Pope ever visited Rome.

Edward II

With the Pope utterly beholden to him, Philip at last had the Templars in his sights. Strangely enough, he had plenty to be grateful to the Templars for. As well as siding with him in his war of words with Boniface, they had loaned him the dowry for his daughter to wed King Edward II of England, and later sheltered him in their Paris temple when the mob rioted for three days.

Despite the debt of gratitude he owed, his intention was to hijack a plan which the Pope had been discussing of merging the Templars and the Hospitallers into a single order called "The Knights of Jerusalem" under the leadership of the Hospitaller

King Edward I of England

Grandmaster, Foulques de Villaret. Philips's idea was to lead the orders himself under the title, "Rex Bellator" or "War King" and hence gain control of the wealth of the combined orders, but with no backers, he settled for the wealth of the Templars. With the death of Edward I and the succession of his weak son, Edward II, at last he would be able to wage a campaign against the English territories in France.

His chief spymaster Philip de Nogaret arranged for sealed orders to be sent all over France, with the strict instructions that they were not to be opened until the morning of Friday 13th October 1307 just in case the Templars had infiltrated his network of secret agents.

De Nogaret had been responsible for the simultaneous arrest of every Jew in France and their mass expulsion without their possessions or property the year before, and was very capable of masterminding an operation that relied on the utmost secrecy for its success.

Meanwhile a campaign of propaganda spread

rumors of blasphemy and sodomy amongst the Templar orders, which appeared to be confirmed when a Templar knight who had been expelled, "confessed" to spitting and trampling on the cross and worshipping a bearded deity called Baphomet.

Jacques de Molay was blissfully unaware of his impending doom as he was accorded the highest honor by King Philip IV who asked him to act as pallbearer for the body of his sister-in-law, Princess Catherine of Valois.

The next day, as the seneschals of France moved to seize the fifteen thousand Templars in France, the pulpits rang with the charges of heresy and sodomy, designed to whip up moral outrage against the order which had hitherto enjoyed popular support. With the Templars in chains, the Dominican Grand Inquisitor went to work on them exacting confessions of blasphemy with torture.

On November 22, the bull Pastoralis Preeminentae went out from Pope Clement V to all Christian monarchs, calling for the Europe-wide arrest and torture of all Templars.

As members of a holy order, they should have been exempt from torture and they must have been utterly dismayed that the only temporal authority to which they were subject, the Holy Mother Church was now ordering that no "known means of torture" should be spared in the investigation of their crimes.

So enthusiastic was the Inquisition that 36 Templars died within the first few days of their arrest. The scale of the operation was such that there were simply not enough traditional instruments of torture, such as the rack and the wheel, to go around, so the method most commonly used was to apply red hot pincers to the skin or to douse the feet in oil and roast them slowly over a fire. As members

Saint Dominic de Guzman

themselves of a holy order, the Inquisitors were forbidden to spill blood, but they got round this imposition with a mixture of imagination and enthusiasm for the work in hand and there were many ingeniously sickening devices for inflicting pain without breaking the skin.

The Congregation of the Holy Office as the Inquisition was formally known, lay for the most part under the control of the Dominicans (Ordo Praedicatorum or Order of Preachers.) Founded by the Spanish priest Dominic Guzman they had cut their teeth in the Albigensian Crusade and pursued and punished heretics with a zeal unmatched by any other order.

Under such duress, it is readily understandable that many Templars confessed to the trumped up charges against them, among which were allegations that they had collaborated with the Moslems to drive the Christians out of the Holy Land. The main drive of the Inquisitors however was to extract confessions of heresy, punishable by the confiscation of property, which was King Philip IV's objective from the beginning. And under the law of the day, once a confession had been made, it was deemed irrevocable, even though we realize now that a man will say anything his interrogators want to hear, just to stop the pain. Worst of all for the Templars, if they subsequently denied the heresy which they had admitted under torture, they were deemed a "relapsed heretic" and the only possible punishment for this was to be burnt at the stake.

Outside France, the Templars fared somewhat better. In Germany the Templar preceptor Hugo of Gumbach, accompanied by twenty knights in full battle armor, stormed into the council of the archbishop of Metz, declaring himself ready to answer to the vile charges of the Pope in the ordeal of trial by combat. Unsurprisingly, no one was ready to take him up on the offer.

In Spain and Portugal, the Templars were too important in the war against the Moslem occupiers to throw away their help so lightly and they were found innocent, so much so that in Portugal, their allegiance was transferred from the Pope to the king and in recognition of their honorable conduct, they were renamed the Knights of Christ.

On April 13th 1312, the Templars were finally disbanded as an order, even though the Pope had balked at the idea of formally condemning as heretical an order, which was beholden unto him alone. So no charges were ever made against the Templars despite the wealth of "evidence" which the Dominican Inquisitors of the Congregation of the Holy Office had found.

In May another bull, Ad Providum, decreed that the entire property of the Templars be transferred to the Hospitallers. Philip IV had to content himself with recouping from that property the expenses incurred for the arrest, torture and imprisonment of the Templars in the four years since their downfall.

Members of the lower ranks who had confessed were allowed to go free, though many of them were broken men. The highest-ranking Templars, including Jacques de Molay, the Grandmaster, were to publicly confess their guilt on a platform especially erected outside the Notre Dame Cathedral in Paris.

As he mounted the steps, he must have known that to retract at this late hour and embarrass the Church would mean an agonizing death, and he was a frail old man over seventy years old,

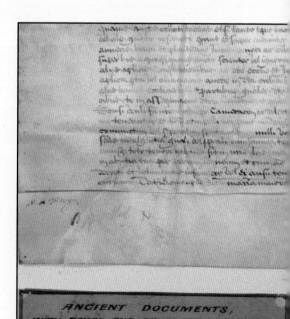

ANCIENT DOCUMENTS,
WITH ROYAL AND OTHER SIGNATURES.
PRESENTED BY
GEORGE E. J. POWELL, ESQ. OF NANTEOS.

who had by now spent over six years in prison. And yet he summoned up the courage to martyr himself when a lesser man would have taken the offer of a pension and somewhere out of the way to spend his remaining years.

Templars being immolated

"I think it only right," he said, when the crowd fell silent, "that at so solemn a moment, when my life has so little time to run, I should reveal the deception which has been practiced and speak up for the truth. Before Heaven and Earth and all of you here as my witnesses, I admit that I am guilty of the grossest iniquity. But the iniquity is that I have lied in admitting the disgusting charges laid against the order. I declare, and I must declare, that the order is innocent. Its purity and saintliness are beyond question. I have indeed confessed that the order is guilty, but I have done so only to save myself from terrible tortures by saying what my enemies wished me to say. Other knights who have retracted their confessions have been led to the stake, yet the thought of dying is not so awful that I shall confess to foul crimes, which have never been committed. Life is offered to me, but at the price of infamy. At such a price, life is not worth living. I do not grieve that I must die if life can be bought only by piling one lie upon another."

As he no doubt foresaw, the revenge of the Church and Crown was swift and cruel. Even as he was bundled off stage, the announcement went out that he would burn for his sins that very evening and every effort would be made to ensure his passing from this world would be as painful as possible.

At public hangings, the executioner could be paid in advance to hang his weight upon the body and thus cause a quick painless death from a broken neck. Likewise, with burning at the stake, the fire could be stoked so that the intense heat consumed the victim very quickly or green boughs could be added to produce smoke which would cause death by smoke inhalation. Potions could be given to render the victim senseless by the time the flames were licking about his body.

King Louis XVI of France

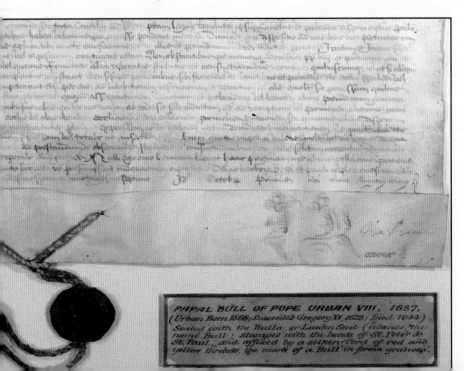

Papal Bull of Pope Urban VIII

Jacques De Molay

But for de Molay, a pyre of dry wood and charcoal would ensure that he was conscious throughout as he was slowly roasted and the pain would be as much as any one man had ever experienced.

As he burned, he cursed King Philip and his family for thirteen generations to come and called for the king and Pope to meet him within the year to answer for their crimes before the throne of God. Clement V was dead before a month was out and Philip died before the end of the year. Legend has it that at the execution of King Louis XVI in the French Revolution, an unidentified man leapt onto the scaffold and began flicking the blood spilt from his severed neck into the crowd, shouting "Jacques de Molay, thou art revenged!"

Meanwhile in England, the Templars had fared rather better than their continental brothers. The weak and ineffectual Prince of Wales had succeeded to the throne three months before the arrest of the Templars in France. Had he been a stronger ruler, he would still have been unwilling to move against the Templars, for the relationship between the Crown and the order was a good one. It was in the grounds of the London Temple, that many of the noble peers of the young Prince spent the night before being knighted at Westminster in preparation for the oncoming war against Robert the Bruce. Many Templars had laid down their lives in the service of his father, Edward I, the most notable being Brian de Jay, Master of the English Temple.

His indecision provided the English Templars with a vital window to make good their plans for escape, for it was not long before word arrived of the dreadful fate of their brothers on the continent.

On December 15th, when he received the papal bull Pastoralis Preeminentae, promulgated on November 22nd, his hand was finally forced. But even then, the orders calling for their arrest did not go out until January 7th and from their announcement in London, they took a while to reach the rest of the country.

Port of La Rochelle

Even in France, despite the utmost secrecy behind the simultaneous arrests, some Templars managed to escape. We know for a fact that none of the eighteen Templar-owned ships in the port of La Rochelle were ever captured and much of the wealth in the Templar treasury, so coveted by Philip IV, had also disappeared.

The English Templars had two months between the arrests in France and the arrival of the papal bull in which to plan their escape. Consequently, when soldiers arrived at the Temple in London, there was no one of significant rank to arrest, all the records had been destroyed and the famed Templar wealth was gone. In all England, only two fugitive Templars were taken. Those who had chosen to stay and face their accusers were treated civilly, permitted to remain under house arrest.

The Inquisition had no authority in England, and although they were allowed to interview the prisoners, they were not permitted to torture them, a situation which infuriated the Pope. Such was his fanatic zeal on the matter that he despatched ten professional torturers from the continent, with words threatening Edward I with excommunication if he did not comply with papal authority. And so, at the instigation of the Church in Rome, the use of torture was permitted for the first time in English jurisprudence.

Perhaps because of the restraint urged by Edward I in the treatment of the Templar prisoners or the fact that they had been incarcerated for two years by then and their resolve was strengthened, no confessions of heresy were extracted. There were many breakouts from prison, which points to collusion and not a single escapee was recaptured, which points to sympathy or at least apathy in the matter of their apprehension.

Needless to say, as soon as the use of torture was instituted in the interrogation of the Templars in England, the stakes became very high for those men on the run.

They were lucky in one respect however. Across the border in Scotland, Robert the Bruce was preparing for war with England. Vastly outnumbered, with a bedraggled yet courageous army, many armed only with farm tools, he was not going to arrest and torture any knights fleeing persecution from the English. With the motto "the enemy of my enemy is my friend" in mind he ignored the papal bull of Pope Clement V and Scotland became a safe haven for the fugitive Templars.

Battle of Bannockburn

According to legend, a group of Templar knights fought alongside Robert the Bruce at the famous Battle of Bannockburn, forming part of the unit of armored cavalry whose role was to break up the ranks of English longbowmen, so deadly on the field.

And so the Templars vanished from the annals of history.

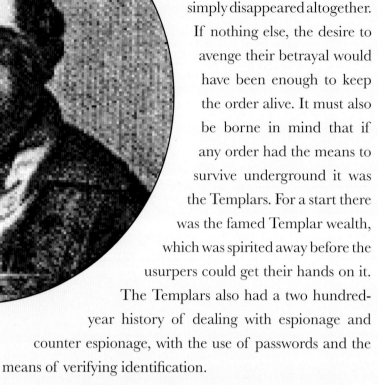

It is difficult to imagine that they simply disappeared altogether. If nothing else, the desire to avenge their betrayal would have been enough to keep the order alive. It must also be borne in mind that if any order had the means to survive underground it was the Templars. For a start there was the famed Templar wealth, which was spirited away before the usurpers could get their hands on it. The Templars also had a two hundred-year history of dealing with espionage and counter espionage, with the use of passwords and the means of verifying identification.

Under the weak and ineffectual rule of Edward I, the country was in a very unstable state. Authority was decentralized and lay in the hands of the lords ordainers, who looked to their own personal gain.

This was the era of Robinhood, when bands of outlaws and robber barons preyed on the conspicuous and ill-gotten wealth of the Church. In fact it is not unreasonable to assume that some of the legends built around noble and virtuous outlaws living in the forests of northern England and

Robert the Bruce

redistributing the wealth of the common people may have been based on stories of fugitive Templars.

Some very persuasive research has been done to suggest that the Templars did indeed survive underground and were the precursors of the secret society that declared itself in 1717 as the Freemasons. It is perhaps no coincidence that many Freemasons regard Scottish Craft Freemasonry as the original and purest form. It is also significant that relations between the Catholic Church and the brotherhood of the Masons has been notoriously antagonistic.

Although it cannot be proved beyond a reasonable doubt, it is just possible that despite the best efforts of King Philip and Pope Clement V, the Templars or at least their legacy continues to exist to this day under the aegis of the biggest fraternal organization the world has ever known.

Coins used by the Templar

chapter 6

To understand the complicated ebb and flow in the fortunes of the Catholic Church in the sixteenth and seventeenth centuries, it is necessary to wind the clock back to the last years of the 1400s.

English Plots

Henry VII

Rich

A new dynasty had been founded when Henry Tudor ascended the throne as Henry VII, having defeated Richard III at the Battle of Bosworth in 1485. Seeking to establish a continent-wide power base, he married his eldest son Prince Arthur to the daughter of King Ferdinand of Aragon and Queen Isabella of Castile, Princess Catherine of Aragon. His other son Henry was set for a career in the Church and his daughters Margaret and Mary were married respectively to King James IV of Scotland and the King of France.

This nexus of alliances seemed to crumble when Prince Arthur died of tuberculosis in 1502. It would have been possible to maintain the alliance with Spain had Prince Henry, who was now heir to the throne, been able

Queen Isabella of Castile

to marry his brother's widow, but the position of the Church of Rome equated marriage to an in-law with incest. However, Henry's father and King Ferdinand did manage to successfully petition the Holy See to have the policy disavowed and within six weeks of the young Henry's succession to the throne, he had married Catherine of Aragon.

Sadly the marriage was not conducive to Henry VIII's dynastic ambitions, for the queen was beset by a series of stillbirths and miscarriages. In 1516, a daughter Mary was born, but Henry was obsessed with continuing the royal line through a male heir. At one stage, it looked as though his wishes had been granted,

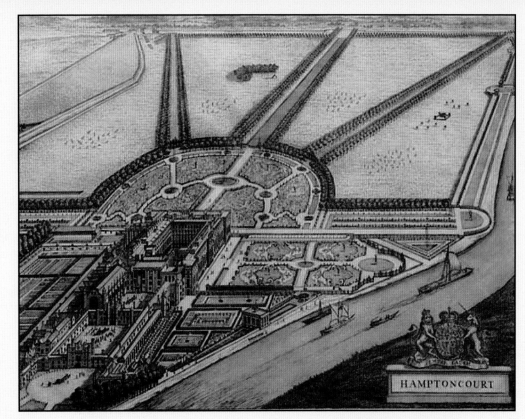

Hampton Court

And Intrigue

but the boy died just over a month later.

Henry's answer was to seek to have the marriage annulled, citing as proof of God's displeasure at his marriage to his brother's widow, the barren state of her womb.

He entrusted this mission to the Lord Chancellor Cardinal Thomas Wolsey, who had made himself very unpopular by using his position to amass a huge personal fortune. Church and state revenues were funnelled into the building of glamorous palaces such as Hampton Court and he had even fathered an illegitimate son,

for whom he secured an annual income of over twenty-seven hundred pounds a year from the sale of Church benefices.

He seemed to embody everything that was corrupt about the Church and his failure to secure papal dispensation for the divorce was the subject of much satisfaction among his many enemies for it ultimately led to his demise.

Annoyed as the Pope may have been at having to reverse the decision made with regard to Catherine of Aragon, he might well have agreed to it had it not been for the presence in Rome of Charles V at the head of a large army. Catherine of Aragon was his aunt and he would not countenance

Catherine of Aragon

Pope Leo X

the annulment of her marriage, which would also have made his cousin, the Princess Mary, illegitimate.

Despite Henry's reputation as the iconoclastic scourge of Rome, he was actually a devout Catholic who had been awarded the title Defender of the Faith by Pope Leo X in recognition of his treatise "In Defense of the Seven Sacraments" written to refute the heretical beliefs of Martin Luther.

Thus, it is erroneous to assume that at the break with Rome, the pendulum immediately swung to the opposite side. Henry was anything but a Protestant. Denying the doctrine of transubstantiation was still punishable by burning at the stake. What he had in mind was very much along the lines of traditional Roman Catholicism, with the crucial difference

that he himself, rather than the Pope in Rome, would stand at its head.

If it had simply been a matter of personal convenience for Henry, he would never have been able to make such a sweeping change, but the whole nation was behind him. The commoners were already alienated by the arrogance of the bishops, who had long since strayed from the simple message of Christianity, with luxurious residences and lifestyles of surfeit and privilege.

As owners of the largest manorial holdings in England, the monastic orders were in effects the overseers of a huge number of "villeins", who were attached to the manor by birth, living in clusters of houses called a "vill." Similar to tenant farmers, they were subject to a great deal of restrictions, the most onerous of which curtailed their freedom of movement.

By becoming the landlord to such a vast percentage of the population, the Church made itself extremely unpopular. Before the Black Death, many villeins had been allowed to purchase their freedom however when the population was decimated by the bubonic plague, labor was at a premium and the Church tried to hold on to this unpaid workforce, by insisting that manumissions be validated and declaring that anyone claiming to be free without proof was simply embezzling Church property. Because of the widespread illiteracy, most villeins had seen no need to procure documentation. The Church also did itself irreparable damage by using parish records to prove that a free man's ancestor had been born a serf and hence he was bound in perpetuity to serfdom.

Many members of the lower clergy were just as hard-pressed and resentful as the villeins because the bishops refused to increase their stipends to meet the rising inflation.

Reformation years before Martin Luther nailed his 95 theses to the door of the castle church at Wittenburg.

His arguments that not only was there no need for an intermediary between man and God, but there was actually no mention of a Pope in the bible proved of invaluable worth to Henry when rallying the country.

As long ago as 1360, John Ball, "the mad priest of Kent" had wondered the country, calling for the landholdings of the Church to be redistributed among the people from whom it had been stolen in the first place. When excommunication did not serve to silence him, he was eventually imprisoned in the Archbishop's dungeons in Maidstone.

Martin Luther

The level of hostility directed against the Church can be gauged by the events of the Peasants' Rebellion in 1381 when Wat Tyler's army marched into Canterbury Cathedral during High Mass and called on the monks to elect a new Archbishop, for they intended to behead the present one.

When they reached London, they sacked his palace in Lambeth and stormed the Tower of London. Finding the Archbishop praying in the chapel, they dragged him to Tower Hill and struck off his head, placing it on a pole on London Bridge for all to see.

It must be borne in mind that early dissenters like John Wycliffe and John Ball did not want to reform the Church. Rather, they wanted to revert to the old principles upon which the early Church had been founded and from which

Men like John Wycliffe sowed the seeds of dissent against what he saw as a hopelessly corrupt Church. He saw the refusal of the Church to sanction a translation of the bible into the vernacular as a means of manipulating the masses and withholding from them the blessings of the teachings of Jesus Christ, which were theirs by right through the miracle of the resurrection.

Overseeing the translation of the Vulgate Bible,

the Roman Church had strayed a long way in the thousand-plus years since it had been founded.

In the first hundred years or so after the foundation of the Church, much of the activity of the Church leaders had been missionary work, which because of the circumstances in which they worked, (remote and dangerous places), was unregulated. As time went on, the bishop of Rome demanded more and more autocratic power over the clergy, reasoning that since he had in effect been entrusted with the keys to the kingdom of Heaven, he was "first among equals" and must be accorded all due respect in ecumenical matters. It was not long before the Popes moved from calling themselves the Vicars of Saint Peter to the Vicars of Christ himself. Pope Gregory had announced in the eleventh century that henceforth only the bishop of Rome could use the title Papa or Pope and all secular rulers must kiss his foot. Boniface VIII went even further in his decree that salvation could only be obtained through the Pope. Hence only his subjects could enter Heaven.

The Church of Rome made itself even more unpopular with the clergy by its position on marriage. Before Pope Urban II, it was not uncommon for priests to be married. Indeed there was sound scriptural basis for their right to marry for at one point in the Gospels Christ casts out demons from Peter's mother-law. Thus they argued, if the founding father of the Church was married why shouldn't they do likewise?

Pope Urban II caused a public relations disaster among his own "outreach workers" by demanding that those members of the clergy who would not obey his injunction to renounce their marriage should have their wives taken and sold into slavery!

There were many in the upper echelons of the Church who realized that this reference to scripture to refute ecclesiastical law set a dangerous precedent. They fully understood that most of the teachings of the Church were the result of clerical reasoning and had drifted from the original message of Christ, which after all was quite simple. This may explain why the move to have the bible translated into the vernacular was seen as so dangerous. If the masses could point to a passage in the Gospels and say that it contradicted what the Pope said, his authority would be seriously compromised.

One of the most contentious issues was based around the idea of the Treasury of Merits, by which it was reasoned that since Christ and the Virgin Mary were so utterly perfect and free from all sin, they had stored up an infinite amount of blessings in the eyes of God. These blessings were held to be accessible to the Pope, who could do with them as he saw fit, even going so far as to sell them.

One might wonder why anyone would want to buy a blessing from the Church, but the practice becomes understandable when placed in conjunction with the notion of Purgatory.

Since only the perfect could enter the Kingdom of Heaven and no man was perfect, the Church invented

Purgatory, where for a set period of time, according to the character of one's life, one would be prepared for Heaven. Buying an "indulgence" from the Church could seriously reduce the amount of time spent in this process and hasten the onset of eternal bliss in the company of the Almighty.

Such a flagrant abuse of the power of the Church had seriously alienated the lower clergy. As for the English barons and earls, they looked with envy at the sheer amount of land that the Church possessed, over one third of the surface of the country. They persuaded Henry that the redistribution of Church estates would guarantee him a loyal following of courtiers. If Henry were to sever the ties with Rome, they argued, it was important to break up these monastic centers as they would without doubt become hotbeds of sedition, conspiring to return the Church to Roman control.

Thomas Cromwell's legislation first paved the way, attacking ecclesiastical abuses, curbing clerical jurisdiction, and abolishing the payment of annates to the Pope. Then by the Act of Supremacy Henry VIII was proclaimed the supreme head of the English Church. The next year, the monasteries were dissolved.

Thomas Cromwell

In the land transfer that followed, the largest since the days of William the Conqueror, Henry cemented his power - base by selling off land to his followers at knockdown prices, thus cleverly assuring that he was not the only one with a vested interest in making the secession permanent.

The Pope's response was to decree that Henry's

Sir Thomas More

subjects were no longer under his protection and that any conqueror of England, even a fellow Christian, could sell the English into slavery. Although this served as useful propaganda for the reformers, Henry was beset by problems.

For a start, there was plenty of opposition to his assumption of the role of head of the Church. The most significant voice of protest came from Sir Thomas More, who had succeeded Wolsey as chancellor in 1529 but resigned three years later in protest at Henry's anti-Roman stance. Arrested after refusing to swear to the new Act of Succession, he was imprisoned and tried for treason. Despite his eloquent and moving defense, he was found guilty on contrived evidence and beheaded. His execution provided a rallying point for those who favored a return to Roman rule.

Henry VIII died when his son was just ten years old. Edward VI's short rule would end just before his sixteenth birthday, but in that brief space of time, England

Edward VI

moved firmly in the direction of Protestantism. He repealed the laws of heresey, regarding the transubstantiation, and oversaw the publication of the Archbishop Cranmer's Book of Common Prayer, which was such a sudden change from the Roman liturgy it provoked an armed rebellion in south-west England.

However, as he lay dying, his protector, the duke of Northumberland, exploited the king's reforming zeal to have his half-sister Mary, who was next in line barred from succession because of her Catholicism. In her place he promoted Lady Jane Grey as heiress who was only fifth in line. She was Northumberland's daughter-in-law and he would have been ruler of England in all but name, were it not for the fact that he lost the support of the council and was arrested for treason nine days after Lady Jane Grey's coronation.

Although he converted to Catholicism, it was a futile attempt to save his life and he was executed. Lady Jane Grey and her husband were initially spared, but after Wyatt's rebellion in 1554, Mary was advised that she would become the focus for Protestant revolution and so they were executed.

Thomas Wyatt had marched into London at the head of 3000 rebels from Kent in protest at Mary's proposed marriage to King Philip II of Spain, intending to place Elizabeth on the throne. Although defeated, it persuaded Mary of the very real threat she faced from the Protestants and in her zeal to defend Roman Catholicism, she would ever afterwards be known as "Bloody Mary."

She had promised religious tolerance, but she soon

Lady Jane Grey 's execution

of the barons and earls who now stood in possession of it.

This was an age when people performed acts of public devotion that were completely at odds with their private faith. It was a dangerous time to wear one's colors on one's sleeve, not the least for Mary's sister Elizabeth, who had mass said in her house every day and made an outward show of Catholicism, all the while secretly adhering to Protestantism.

Ultimately however, Mary completely misjudged the country's long-standing rivalry with Spain in her determination to have her husband reign as King of England, despite advice that he should remain the prince consort. Her relationship with King Philip drew England into war with France, as a result of which Calais, the last English possession on the continent was lost.

Dying without producing a male Catholic heir, the throne passed to Elizabeth. Because of her great circumspection, the country assumed she would follow in her sister's footsteps, but as she became more confident of her position and the support around her, her true convictions emerged.

The Pope, naturally enough, was furious and excommunicated her, declaring that her Catholic subjects owed her no allegiance. As she reinstated the anti-Roman laws and made Protestantism the national faith, her Catholic enemies plotted her downfall.

In 1568, her cousin Mary Queen of Scots sought refuge in England. As a potential Catholic claimant to the throne, plots fomented around her and she was kept prisoner in the Tower although Elizabeth was reluctant to have her executed

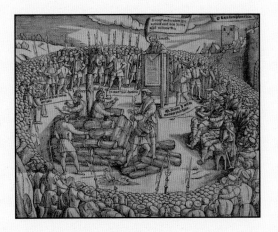

showed her true colors, re-enacting the old heresy laws and ecclesiastical courts. Restoring the English Church to the supremacy of Rome, she equated heresy with treason and in her brief reign executed over three hundred Protestants.

She burnt the Anglican bishops Latimer and Ridley at the stake in 1555, and Archbishop Cranmer met the same fate a year later. She made a small token gesture of mercy to these men of the cloth by allowing them to wear sacks of gunpowder around their necks to hasten their demise!

All married clergy were removed from their benefices, Cardinal Pole arrived in England as papal legate and absolved the country from schism, a synod restored Catholic doctrine and ceremonial, but Mary knew that to returning the monastic property would lose her the support

Anglican Bishops Latimer and
Ridley being burnt at the Stake

Elizabeth I

Spain, he intended to kill Elizabeth and place Mary on the throne. Because the plot was discovered while Ridolfi was abroad, he escaped arrest but the duke of Norfolk was executed for his part.

Another conspiracy to overthrow Elizabeth centered around Francis Throckmorton, son of Sir John Throckmorton who was involved in the rebellion of Sir Thomas Wyatt against Bloody Mary, and nephew of Sir Nicolas Throckmorton, the chamberlain of the exchequer and later ambassador to France. Sir Nicolas himself had been suspected of involvement in the plot to arrange the marriage of the duke of Northumberland to Mary Queen of Scots and spent some time imprisoned in Windsor Castle before proceedings were dropped.

Francis had come under Roman Catholic influence at Oxford and when he was later called to the bar, he joined a circle of sympathisers at the Inner Temple in London, who hid and supported the first Jesuit missionaries to England.

In 1583, he became the principal English agent of a plot that originated in France to invade England, restore papal authority and free Mary Queen of Scots. The invasion force was to have been led by Henry duc de Guise, with Spanish military support, but after Francis had taken a house on Paul's Wharf in London, he began to arouse the suspicion of the counter-espionage agents and in November 1583, he was arrested. Before being carted off to the Tower, he managed to have a bundle of compromising correspondence and a letter in code sent to the Spanish ambassador Mendoza, but he could not hold out under torture on the rack and confessed all. As a result, the Spanish ambassador was expelled and the political situation became very tense indeed.

It wasn't until it was revealed just how close the Babington plot came to overthrowing Elizabeth that she

despite the advice of her privy council.

In 1569, the Catholic earls of northern England led a rebellion. Although eventually quelled by government troops, the armed uprising calling for the restoration of Catholicism demonstrated just how easily the country could be engulfed by civil war.

The leader of the rebellion, Thomas Howard, duke of Norfolk, who almost immediately submitted to Elizabeth, was later implicated in a plot to assassinate her known as the Ridolfi plot, after the Italian banker Roberto Ridolfi who operated out of London. With the support of Catholic

was finally persuaded to authorize Mary's execution for high treason.

Secretly brought up Catholic, as a youth Anthony Babington had served as page boy to the earl of Shrewsbury, keeper of Mary Stuart, to whom he became devoted. In 1580 he attended Elizabeth's court in London, at the same time making contact with the secret society that was supporting the Jesuit missionaries. On a trip to Paris, he became involved with Mary's supporters, and he was entrusted with letters for her on his return. The conspiracy to overthrow the government began to take shape around 1586 and had the support of King Philip of Spain, who promised an armed force to help in the difficult times following the Elizabeth's assassination.

Unfortunately for them both, Mary had been led into thinking there was a safe way of communicating with Babington, when in actual fact all their letters were being intercepted. Foolishly, he put his plans into writing, believing the code he used to be unbreakable.

However Elizabeth's "spymaster" Sir Francis Walsingham was a genius at subterfuge. Way ahead of his time in espionage, he had trained his agents in creating false handwriting, breaking and repairing seals without detection and he had on his payroll the master cryptographer Thomas Phelippes. Phelippes used a technique known as frequency analysis to break Babington's code, which was a rather basic letter substitution. By examining which letters occurred most frequently he could assume they represented the letters that occur most frequently in English and thus the content could be reached through a combination of trial and error and educated guesswork.

One of Babington's co-conspirators, John Ballard, was seized and confessed to everything under torture. Babington, unaware he had been exposed, had applied

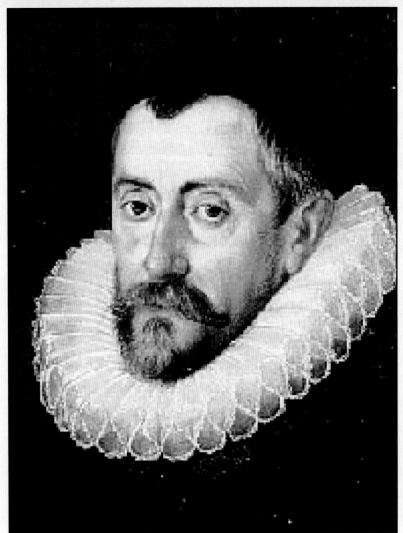

Francis Walsingham

for a passport to travel abroad with the stated purpose of spying on the exiled Catholics, but with the actual intention of finalising the arrangements.

The story goes that one of Walsingham's servants unwittingly allowed him to see a memorandum ordering his arrest and he fled in disguise to Harrow, where he was hidden by a Roman Catholic convert. Meanwhile, the ports were closed. When he was discovered, he offered £1000 for his pardon, a huge sum in those days, but he was executed in Lincoln's Inn Fields.

The postscript of one of Mary's letters was cited as proof that she knew of Babington's plot, but there is some controversy as to whether this was added to expedite her death, for she had become not just an embarrassment but a very real political and personal threat to Elizabeth.

However the danger did not pass with the death of

her cousin. King Philip of Spain was determined to oust the Protestant Queen. Striking at England would deal a double blow, both at a ruler who espoused a heretical perversion of Church teachings and at a country whose recent naval successes by men like Drake, Hawkins, Grenville and Raleigh had seriously hampered his activity in the Americas.

When his planned invasion of England failed and his ships were blown off course round the north of Scotland, the anti-Roman population saw his failure to return the nation to the control of Rome as evidence of God's favorable view of Protestantism and indeed the gale that broke up the Spanish Armada was afterwards known as the "Protestant Gale."

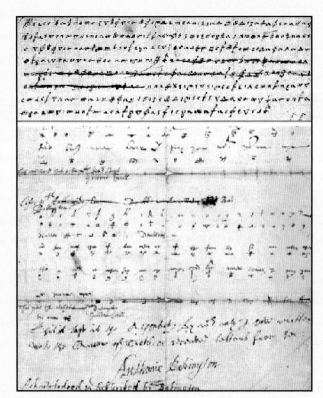

Babington postscript
(Code)

With the threat from Spain dealt with, Catholic hopes of subjecting the crown to papal authority centered on the covert activity of the Jesuits, who made it their business to remove Elizabeth from the throne "by any means necessary." They looked on England in the same way they regarded any potentially dangerous missionary work in a nation of non-believers, with the difference that there was an existing underground network of Catholics intent on toppling the monarchy, with which to liase and provide leadership and direction. Many of these Soldiers of Christ were experts in the art of subterfuge, concealing their identity with disguises and using complex codes to communicate with one another.

They had to be constantly on their guard, for this was the age of the "priest-hunter." Some of the Jesuits were employed by noble families who made an outward show of Protestantism but had the Catholic mass performed in private. Should the authorities come knocking, they often had the use of a "priest-hole" in which to hide. One such designer of these ingenious contraptions, Nicolas Owen, was even canonized by the Church in 1970, over three hundred years after he was tortured and executed for what was regarded as a treasonable offence.

The efforts of the Jesuits were made all the more urgent in that England was drifting further and further away from Anglicanism, which resembled Roman Catholicism in most respects save for rejection of papal supremacy, towards Puritanism, in which the ornamentation and ritual were completely removed.

Even the Holy Sacrament of the Eucharist was under threat, for it had come to represent the arrogance of the Roman Catholic bishops. The vaunted ability to command God is summed up by Father John A. O'Brien in his "The Faith of Millions: the Credentials of the Catholic Church."

"The supreme power of the priestly office is the power of consecrating. "No act is greater" says saint Thomas, "than the consecration of the body of Christ." In this essential phase of the sacred ministry, the power of the priest is not surpassed by that of the bishop, the archbishop, the cardinal or the Pope. Indeed, it is equal to that of Jesus Christ himself. For in this role the priest speaks with the voice and authority of God himself.

"When the priest pronounces the tremendous words of consecration, he reaches up into the heavens, brings Christ down from his throne, and places him upon our altar to be offered up again as the victim for the sins of man. It is a power greater than that of monarchs and emperors; it is greater than that of saints and angels, greater than

ɔim

that of Seraphim and Cherubim. Indeed, it is even greater than then power of the Virgin Mary; for while the Blessed Virgin was the human agency, by which Christ became incarnate a single time, the priest brings Christ down from heaven, and renders Him present on our altar as the eternal victim for the sins of man - not once but a thousand times! The priest speaks and lo! Christ, the eternal and omnipotent God, bows his head in humble obedience to the priest's command."

Less than two years after the accession of James VI of Scotland following Elizabeth's death in 1603, the biggest Catholic plot of them all was discovered.

ɔhim

The brains and driving force behind the conspiracy was Robert Catesby. As a youth, he had seen his father maltreated and imprisoned for refusing to adopt the doctrine of the Church of England and this had inspired him to dedicate his life to the overthrow of the government. Long before the Gunpowder plot, he had been involved in the abortive revolt of the earl of Essex against Elizabeth. Indeed, he had spent time in prison for his part and was only released upon payment of a substantial fine. This brought him to the attention of the authorities and he was picked up again for sending secret agents to Spain to plan an invasion of England.

When King James came to the throne, he promised a more tolerant attitude to the Catholics, but Catesby was already plotting to eradicate the Protestant ruling class by blowing up Parliament. For the time being, he kept his plans

James VI of Scotland

to himself, but when King James reneged on his promise by banishing Catholic priests, Catesby began to gather a core of conspirators around himself.

His cousin Thomas Winter was the first person he let in on the plot and by May 1604, Thomas Percy, John Wright and Guy Fawkes, a soldier from the Netherlands brought in for his knowledge of explosives, had also been involved.

Catesy knew that if at one fell swoop he killed the king, the queen, prince Henry, the privy council and the members of Parliament, all of whom would be present at the opening of Parliament after the summer recess, the way would be open for a Catholic coup to seize power.

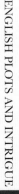

The Gunpowder Plot
being hatched

In the early summer of 1604, the five conspirator rented a house adjoining Parliament and began to dig a tunnel underground to a point beneath the chamber of the House of Lords. The ground was hard and the going slow and by March the plan was abandoned when a cellar came up for rent, which was next to the cellar beneath the Palace of Westminster.

It was quite a simple matter to open up a passageway between the two spaces and Fawkes proceeded to bring in twenty barrels of gunpowder. He placed a quantity of iron bars on top of them to act as shrapnel and covered the lot with coals and bundles of firewood.

The first day of Parliament was due in October but did not take place until November 5th. In the meantime, the conspirators went their separate ways and laid low. Catesby planned a hunting trip to coincide with the explosion at which he intended to gather a host of Catholic gentry, who would lead the country in the wake of the power vacuum created by the explosion. He also planned to capture the younger son of King James, Prince Charles and his sister Princess Elizabeth, and place one or other on the throne.

The course of English history might well have been changed forever on November 5th had it not been for the fact that Catesby chose to involve more people in his plot. The need for money and horses was probably the reason why he felt he could not continue with only four helpers. This proved a fatal error for among the thirteen conspirators was Francis Tresham, whose brother-in-law, Lord Monteagle, as a member of the House of Lords, would die in the planned explosion.

There were indeed a number of Catholics who would have died, but Catesby was against the idea of warning them not to attend Parliament for fear that the plot would fail. Tresham sent word to his brother-in-law warning

Guy Fawkes

him to "retire yourself into the country, for though there be no appearance of any stir, yet I say they shall receive a terrible blow this Parliament and yet they shall not see who hurts them."

Sending the letter to the earl of Salisbury, the king's chief minister, a search of the Westminster Palace cellar subsequently discovered the gunpowder, and Guy Fawkes who was on the scene was apprehended.

The agonies of the rack soon proved too much to endure and he revealed all the names of the conspirators. Catesby and three others fled to the countryside and hid out in a safe-house. But during the flight their gunpowder had got wet and they foolishly tried to dry it next to the fire. Alerted by the explosion, soldiers soon surrounded the house and all four men were killed trying to break out.

Upon hearing of the plot the nation erupted in a wave of anti-Catholic hysteria, burning effigies of the Pope on top of huge bonfires, a practice which survives in England to this day, although the figure is now "the guy", representing Guy Fawkes.

When King James died, Charles I showed an extraordinary lack of understanding of the troubles his predecessors faced by marrying Princess Henrietta Maria of France, who was a devout Catholic. Naturally, the court filled up with a number of foreign Catholics and the barons and parliamentarians became very edgy.

ARREST OF GUY FAWKES.

His chief religious adviser Archbishop Laud angered the Puritans who dominated parliament by reintroducing ornamentation and ritual to the English Church and even provoked an armed revolt in Scotland. Charles blundered on, by claiming that both the Church and the Army were under his, not parliament's, control and hence he could do with them as he saw fit. He then outraged public sentiment by entering parliament with an armed guard to arrest five members.

The ultimate result was civil war and he paid for it with his life, mounting the scaffold in front of his palace in Whitehall on January 30th 1649 and placing his head on the executioner's block before a huge crowd.

England under Oliver Cromwell was a dour and gloomy place, with virtually every form of entertainment regarded as sinful. When his son took over as Lord Protector, he lacked the leadership and determination his father had shown and the army deposed him and invited Charles' son to return from exile in France, little knowing that he was a secret Catholic.

Charles II knew full well from his father's fate that he had to tread carefully. Thus he proceeded very cautiously, working to create a more tolerant atmosphere, in which the religious persecutions of the past would have no place. He devoted much time and energy trying to prevent the proposal that only Anglican Catholics be eligible for service in the government.

However, despite his moderate and pacifistic stance, there were still rumors that he had done a deal with the King of France, whereby he would gradually ensure the return of England to the supremacy of Rome in return for a significant amount of money. These suspicions seemed to be confirmed in 1988 when Lord Clifford of Chudleigh released some of his family's archival records and a signed letter from the king promising payment of 1.2 million livres was unearthed.

Things came to a head in 1666 with the Great Fire of London, when the rumor went about that the fire had been started by Catholics, as a preliminary strike against the seat of government. One of the King's mistresses, Nell Gwynn, was even waylaid by an angry mob and only managed to calm the mood by exclaiming "Why good people, I am the Protestant whore!"

Charles II's circumspection continued right up until his death when the last rites were administered by a Catholic priest who had to be smuggled up the back stairs.

Nell Gwynn

The tide soon turned back the other way with the succession of his brother James II, who was a devout Catholic and not afraid to show it. Charles II's courtiers had tried to persuade him to nominate his illegitimate but Protestant son, the Duke of Monmouth, but to no avail. Their fears of persecution were fulfilled when James II used the failed invasion of Monmouth as an excuse to suppress the Catholics. Those who had helped the rebel troops were dealt with very severely, being branded, executed and even sold into slavery. Protestant admirals and generals were replaced with Catholics and religious freedom was proclaimed.

When the Archbishop of Canterbury and six other bishops refused to preach this message of freedom from the pulpit, James II prosecuted them but lost the case. In the end, his zealous efforts to return England to Rome only managed to unite all the Protestant sects together. For the time being, it seemed as though his mission would die with him as there was no heir, so the secret societies that flourished were playing a waiting game. However, in June 1688, his wife gave birth to a baby boy and the king announced to the nation's horror that he would be educated by the hated Jesuits. At this, the Protestant propaganda machine went into overdrive, spreading the rumor that the succession was a Jesuit plot and the boy had in fact been smuggled into the royal bedchamber in a warming pan!

But there was only so much a smear campaign could achieve and soon it was decided that action was needed. A group of Protestant leaders, among them the Bishop of London, asked James II's daughter, Mary, and her husband William of Orange, who were the next in line to the throne after the baby, to take the crown. William was a devout Protestant who proved his mettle by defeating King Louis XIV of France in the Grand war of Alliance. Offering little resistance, James II fled to France and in the "Glorious

Revolution," William and Mary were crowned king and queen.

In 1689 a law was passed that excluded Roman Catholics from the throne but this did not put an end to all the plotting. William had made a serious enemy of the Catholic clans in Scotland by requiring that they present themselves to sign a pledge of allegiance to the crown. The chief of one of the branches of the MacDonald clan from the Glencoe valley missed the deadline because of a severe winter storm. To punish this intransigence, Captain Robert Campbell of Glenlyon and his troops slaughtered forty men, women and children.

Since the throne was denied to James II and his son by law, their supporters, known as the Jacobites, began to plot how to take it by force. Such was their hatred of William that when his horse tripped on a molehill and crushed him to death, the Jacobites remembered the mole with the toast: "To the little gentleman in black velvet."

The crown passed to his daughter Queen Anne, a strict Protestant, who could not provide a male heir despite seventeen pregnancies.

An attempt by the Jacobites to crown James II's son as James III in London so provoked the citizens that those taking part had to flee for their lives. Parliament then moved to ensure that the crown would never return to Roman Catholic hands by passing the Act of Succession, which decreed that after Anne's death the crown must pass to the nearest Protestant relative of the House of Stuart.

Meanwhile James Edward Stuart, known as the Old Pretender attempted to invade Scotland, reaching the Firth of Forth with 5,000 men but he went away empty-handed. Seven years later in 1715, he returned, after the Earl of Mar in Scotland and the English Jacobite, the Earl of Dentwater, started a revolt. He landed at Peterhead, having himself proclaimed James VII of Scotland and James III of England and marched south to Scone. However, his nerve failed and his Highland troops deserted on the approach of the Earl of Argyle. Two years later, he suffered another spectacular setback when a Spanish naval expedition was scattered by a storm, only two battered frigates reaching as far as the Hebrides.

It must have been galling for him to see the crown pass to the Hanoverian dynasty, with King George I, who never even bothered to learn English and spent more time in Germany than in England. One year after the failure of the Spanish mission, his wife gave birth to a son in Rome, where they were living as guests of the Holy See. The boy would grow up to be the Romantic figure known as Bonnie Prince Charlie, the last great hope of the Jacobite cause.

He was toasted by many a Scotsman and English Jacobite, who could not mention him by name for to do so was a treasonable offence. Instead, they passed their glass over a bowl of water, shouting "To the King!" by which they did not mean King George but "The King over the water!"

Bonnie Prince Charlie could count on the help of the Catholic enemies of England, in particular England's arch-rival France and indeed, the King put a fleet of 7,000 men at his disposal ready to sail from Calais, but they were prevented from sailing by violent storms and the appearance of a huge squadron of English warships.

And so, the Young Pretender sold all his jewels and bought two armed frigates and set sail from France with a

Bonnie Prince Charlie

Battle on Culloden Moor

But the further they marched from Scotland the more over-stretched they became and British troops had been ordered back from the continent to meet the threat.

The Final defeat came at the battle on Culloden Moor in 1746 where the Jacobite cause was effectively ended. As a political force they were finished as was any hope of returning the throne to the dominion of Rome.

few Scottish patriots. In the campaign which followed, the course of British history was very nearly irrevocably altered, for almost the entire British army was in Flanders fighting the French.

He was able to muster a considerable force of fearsome Highland warriors and the English Commander-in-Charge foolishly left the way open to invade England from the north. At one point it even looked as though they might take London.

chapter 7

Most of the major European countries either expelled or massacred their Jewish populations at some point in the early medieval period (England 1290, France 1306, Spain 1391 and 1492, Germany 1348). The Jews were seldom allowed to leave with more than they could carry on their backs. These were often thinly veiled attempts to raise money by selling off property and possessions and cancelling debts incurred by the crown, but with a veneer of respectability that came with official church sanction. The reintroduction of the Inquisition in Spain in 1478 during the Reconquista was especially arduous for the Jews, all the more so as life under the Spanish Moors was noted for its tolerance.

The Phantom Judaic-
Masonic Plots And

The antagonism of the early Roman Church towards the Jewish Diaspora seems to stem from the fact that the Jews represented a threat to its divinely ordained authority. Because Judaism does not recognize Christ as the Messiah, it follows that it will not admit that through Christ and on through Peter, each Pope is the successive agent of divine will on Earth. The Pope says that the only way to God is through the Church, but the Jews bypass this route to salvation with their own beliefs and ritual. Everyone else has to confess their sins to the priest and ask his forgiveness. The Jews have their own way of dealing with sin and atonement.

For a Church, which is constantly seeking to stamp its authority on the population, the Jews represent a real problem. But there may well be another reason.

There is a real contradiction between the many pronouncements of the Church that the Jews

Roman Catholic Church

are doomed to wander the earth, a pariah people who are perpetually punished for the ultimate sin of having killed the Son of God, and the scriptural injunction that the sins of the fathers shall not be visited on the sons.

Much of the recent research, into the life and times of Christ has focussed on the probability that Christ's death was sought by the Romans and not by the Jews. After all, crucifixion was a form of execution reserved exclusively for the enemies of Rome. Biblical scholars have also pointed out the fact that the New Testament was written for a Graeco-Roman audience and hence the role of the Romans in Jesus' death was deliberately downplayed to make Christianity

Pope Paul IV

The Loss Of The Papal States

more palatable. Hence the transferal of blame for Christ's death onto the Jews.

Is it thus possible that the reason the Roman Catholic Church was so vituperative in its condemnation of Jews and Judaism, constantly reiterating their role in the murder of Christ, was because they wanted to eradicate the connection between this act of deicide and a Church that lies in the heart

of the Roman Empire, at whose head stands a descendent of those Roman citizens?

Before Pope Paul IV, the Jews in the Papal State's had lived much like the rest of the population, with relative freedom to travel and earning their livelihood as they saw fit. All that all changed however in 1555, with the promulgation of his first papal bull which prohibited Jews from owning land or property and taking part in any economic activity other than selling rags.

Furthermore they were to be confined within the bounds of a ghetto, with high walls and gates that were locked at night. Not only were these ghettos cramped and overcrowded with narrow streets and ramshackle houses, they were often built in noisy parts of the city, near meat markets and sewers, and in the case of Rome's ghetto on banks of the Tiber which regularly flooded.

It may surprise the reader to know that the Nazis were not the first to make the Jewish population wear a badge of identity. Under the terms of the 1555 dict, "Jews

of both sexes must wear a yellow-colored sign, by which they are distinguished from others, and they must always wear it at all times and places, both in the ghettos and when they are outside them."

Needless to say Paul IV was not the most popular of Popes and when he died in 1559 Jews and Christians united in celebration. The palace of the hated Inquisition was looted and a statue of the Pope pulled off its plinth, (in much the same way the effigy of Saddam Hussein was toppled) and a yellow hat placed on his head by a Jew as the crowds cheered.

The early eighteenth century was marked by a more tolerant atmosphere in which the restrictions on travel and employment were somewhat relaxed. Compared with his successor Clement XIV was a benign reformer. Jews were allowed to practice medicine and open factories outside the ghetto (there was no room inside). In 1769 he had agreed to disband the Jesuits, who were regarded as little better than papal spies and in 1773 he took the Roman ghetto out of the hands of the hated Inquisitors and replaced them with the office of the cardinal vicar.

However when Pius VI came to the Throne of Peter in 1775, it was immediately clear that he intended to reintroduce the most draconian measures of 1555, which forbade the Jew even from riding in a horse-drawn carriage "lest he think himself above a Christian he passes going on foot."

Pope Piu

There was also a concerted attempt on behalf of the Vatican to keep Jews from mixing with Christians. Hence the directive that: "The Jews may not play, nor eat, nor drink, nor have any other familiarity or conversation with Christians, nor Christians with Jews, whether in buildings, houses, or vineyards, nor on the street, or in inns, taverns, stores or elsewhere."

Jews praying at the Synagogue on Yom Kippur

There was also a ban on hiring Christian domestic help. "Jews cannot keep male or female servants, nor make use of them even for the briefest moment, nor employ them to clean the ghetto, nor to light their fire, nor wash their clothes, nor to do any task for them."

It had been common practice to hire Christians to light fires on the Sabbath as the Jews were not permitted to do so by the tenets of their religion. Several prominent members of society complained that not only was this uncharitable to the Jews for in the winter their children and old folk would suffer terribly as a consequence, it was also punitive to the Christian charwomen for whom this was a much-needed source of revenue.

The Vatican however was implacable and went even further in its effort to ensure that "good Christians" would not be contaminated by contact with the superstitions of the Jewish population, hence the ban on Christians entering synagogues. In a patently systematic attempt to erase all trace of their faith, Jews were forbidden to use religious accoutrements or ritual when transporting coffins to the cemetery and even their tombstones were to be left blank.

Perhaps the most onerous burden of the new pontiff's reforms lay in the practice of "forced sermons", whereby every Saturday afternoon at the close of the Sabbath service a revolving list of Jews were summoned from the ghetto to sit in the pews and listen in respectful silence while the priest badmouthed their religion. Worse still it was the delight of the mob to hurl abuse at them and in the winter their humiliation was compounded by being pelted with snowballs.

There was some relief from their plight when in 1796 the theories of the enshrined in the Declaration of the Rights of Man and of the Citizen, came to the Papal States with Napoleon's forces. Upholding the principles that "all men are born free and equal in rights" with the right to ownership of property, freedom of movement and equality before the law, the French troops tore down the gates of the ghettos and liberated the Jews.

In February 1798 Rome fell and Pius IV was forced into exile. The occupation did not last long however, ending just before the turn of the century when forces from Naples pushed back the French. Just as suddenly as they had arrived they were gone, and with them went the advances the Jews had made.

Less than a decade later, Napoleon's forces briefly returned and for a while it looked as though the Jewish situation might improve but the Napoleonic Empire did not last too long and finally collapsed in 1814.

One thing that went in the Jews' favor was the election of Ercole Consalvi to the position of secretary of state to Pope Pius VII. An exceptionally talented diplomat he had a reforming zeal, which was absolutely unique in the Vatican at that time. He was alone in realizing that the French Revolution had changed the world forever. Gone were the days when the populace would accept the divinely ordained right of the Church and Crown to hold sway without question.

"I have talked myself hoarse, in vain", he wrote "saying that the Revolution has done to politics and morality what the Flood did to physics, changing the entire face of the earth... Trying to make people reflect on the fact that simply saying that this or that thing wasn't done before, and that our laws are fine as they are, and one shouldn't change anything, are errors of the most serious sort... If we set out on the wrong path, if we commit some irremediable mistake, we won't keep the lands we have regained for more than six months. I wish to God what lies in the future will not confirm this prophecy, but unfortunately it is just what will happen if we take any false steps."

His calls for reform however were met just as vociferously by the hard-liners, or zelanti, as they were known

The Insignia of Pius VII

within the Vatican. Chief among them was Giuseppe Sala who had submitted a plan for papal reform to Pius VII, in which great stress was laid on the advances which had been

made by the Jews and the necessity of reversing them.

Consalvi had realized that the position of the Vatican with regard to the Jews was a dangerous anachronism, a throwback to the medieval days, which could be used by the enemies of the Church to remove still more power from them. Already the Church looked ridiculously out of step with modern times and the principles of equality that were being promoted all over Europe and in America.

In reply to a letter from the papal delegate to Ferrara asking what should be done with the Jews he replied,

"Putting the Jews back in their old state of servitude… would produce the most disgusting political and indeed economic consequences. Should the Jews see themselves treated this way, they would leave the Papal States."

The Jews in the northern states were confident that the rights they had won would remain. They were in Austrian hands and it was doubtful at first whether they would be returned to Papal control. It was almost two decades since the days of the ghettos and many of the young men had grown up without any interference in their lives from the Church. When it became clear that the Legations, as these territories were known, would be handed back the Austrian Government let it be known that they expected the Jews to keep the rights they had won.

"They should be allowed to exist without fear of being sent back to that precarious, vilified state in which they found themselves near the end of the past century, leaving them instead in peace to enjoy that civil status which their civilization and the liberal sentiments of the European courts have procured for them over the past twenty years."

Consalvi was however fighting a losing battle by now for the Inquisition, abolished by the French, which was already reinstated in Rome. Jewish students had been

Although Clement IX had put a stop to the custom, by which Jews were forced to run naked from the Arch of Domitian to the Church of St. Mark while the crowds pelted them with missiles and the Pope looked on from his balcony, in 1779 Pius VI had brought back the equally odious Lenten tradition of making the rabbis march out from the ghetto dressed in ridiculous outfits to make obeisance to the Roman authorities.

There was brief respite under the French but the days of tolerance were over. There was a general feeling

Lenten Carnival

St. Mark

The Insignia of Clement IX

CLEMENTE IX

Holy Communion for Baptism

among the cardinals that the Jews had benefited in direct proportion to the setbacks that the Church suffered under the Napoleonic occupation and now that the French forces were gone it was payback time.

Around this time the issue of forced baptisms came to a head. It was not uncommon for young Jewish men to seek a way out of the ghetto by converting to Christianity. Only then would they have the freedom to live and travel where they wanted and engage in any trade they saw fit. To do so they came to the House of the Catechumens near the Coliseum, where they would have to stay for the next forty days while they received religious instruction and the baptismal rite. However if they were married, they would also have to pledge their wife and children to the Church as a sign of commitment.

Often, the first time a wife knew about her husband's conversion was when the criminal magistrate of the vicariate, accompanied by the police, knocked on the door late at night and entered with a legally-binding warrant for their incarceration.

For the Holy See, forced conversions were not an attempt to humiliate the Jews. The Church was sincere albeit rather misguided in its belief that this was the only chance the Jews had of being saved. Each conversion was a little victory over the Devil who had led the Jews into ignorant superstition and as such confirmed the divinely ordained supremacy of the Roman Catholic Church. Thus they were tremendously important public relations opportunities and occasionally the Pope himself would personally administer the baptism at the end of the preliminary period of study.

It was also widely believed within the Church that the acceptance of Christ by the children of Israel was a sign of the Second Coming and hence each conversion hastened the return of the Messiah.

Sometimes the enforced isolation and the pressure brought to bear by the priests and nuns would eventually sway the wife and she might give in, more often than not at the end of the required time she would plead to be returned to her people. However if her child had already been baptized by the priest, she would not be allowed to take him with her, for in the eyes of the Church to do so would be to abandon the child, which had received the Holy Spirit and was now one of God's children, to torment among the godless pagans.

There were several prominent cases of forced conversion in the early nineteenth century, which generated great sympathy for the Jews and caused an outcry against the high-handed behavior of the Roman Church.

In one case a Christian widow had gone to the Roman ghetto to make some purchases. She fell into conversation with a young Jewish woman with an ailing child. When this woman left the girl in the widow's care to fetch her groceries, she sprinkled some water from a well over the child's head and administered the baptismal rite. As she later explained

Coat of Arms of Livorno

to her confessor, the child looked so sick that she thought she would ensure its soul was saved were it to die.

On hearing of this the confessor took the matter to the Holy Office of the Inquisition and soon enough Pope Pius IV himself was involved and authorized the seizure of the child, even though it was not yet clear whether a valid baptism had taken place. Six months later, while the child was still in the care of the House of the Catechumens it was decided that the baptism was genuine. Since to return her to the ghetto would mean that she would abandon her faith, and then be guilty of apostasy, which was one of the worst sins imaginable it was decided she must stay.

Another example concerned a young man who had come to the Catechumens and converted but had since changed his mind and disappeared. When he was traced to Livorno in the grand duchy of Tuscany it was discovered that he had married and his wife was now eight months pregnant. The grand duchy officials were initially unwilling to arrest the couple but the rector of the Catechumens, who seems to have made it his personal mission to see the absconding Jew returned, appealed to the Papal secretary of state. Although the husband could not be found, his wife was discovered in Pisa and she was arrested.

When she gave birth the child was taken from her and baptized on the grounds that even though its father was an apostate he was still a Christian and therefore the marriage was invalid in the eyes of Church law.

Sometimes a Christian nurse caring for a dying Jew might secretly administer the baptism and then when his family came to collect the body they would be told that as a Christian he could not be buried in the Jewish cemetery. In 1820 a board of Church theologians ruled that the body of a baby Jewish girl could not be released to her parents when she died two days after birth because the Christian midwife had baptized her. Amid a storm of protest the girl was buried in consecrated ground.

Perhaps the most flagrant abuse of the power of the House of the Catechumens occurred in 1823 while the conclave was in session to elect the new Pope after the death of Pius VII.

Location of the conclave

Pellegrino Toscano asked the rector to accept his offer of converting. He pledged his wife who was six months pregnant and the rector sent for authorization to have her brought to the Catechumens. However in the next twenty-four hours Toscano had a change of heart and retracted his offer.

Imagine his surprise, therefore, when the rector told him that it was too late to withdraw and when his wife gave birth the child would be baptized. The only way she could keep it would be to be baptized herself.

When his wife refused to eat the hospital food because it was not kosher, the cardinal vicar, fearful of the outrage should she suffer a miscarriage as a result of her confinement, allowed her to return to the ghetto on the strict instructions that the moment the baby was born, it should be given up to the Christian midwife who was to oversee the delivery.

There was further uproar when an eighty-year-old man clearly suffering the effects of dementia pledged his wife and his granddaughter to the Catechumens. Although his son had no desire whatsoever to convert to Christianity, the four year-old-girl was removed from her parents and brought up as a ward of the monastery.

Cases such as these made the Vatican extremely unpopular and undoubtedly contributed to the losses the Papal States would suffer over the next half century.

When Pius VII died in 1823, the rivalry intensified between those seeking to modernize the Roman Church and those who did all in their power to thwart their efforts. Consalvi, the reforming secretary of state under Pius VII had the backing of the courts of Austria, France and Spain, which had the right to block the election of one candidate, so long as they did so before he had received a two thirds majority.

When it looked like Antonio Severoli was going to win, they used their veto to block him but in response the zelanti regrouped and proposed another hardliner, Annibale della Genga, the cardinal vicar of Rome, described by the Archbishop of Westminster as "tall and emaciated, weak in his gait, and pallid in countenance, as if he had just risen from a bed of sickness, to pass within to that of death."

Annibale della Genga

It immediately became clear what direction the papacy would take under his guidance. Taverns were no longer to be permitted to sell alcohol, public statues of naked women were removed and statues of naked men had their genitals "excised" by stone masons. Any man deemed to be walking too close behind a woman was to be seized and thrown in jail and the playing of and dancing to the waltz was made illegal. Unsurprisingly he was greeted with ridicule when he appeared in public and so he lived the life of a recluse.

The ridicule soon turned into something more serious however as the hardline reforms continued apace. Underground revolutionary cells plotted the overthrow of the papacy and in Ravenna alone Agostino Cardinal Rivarola oversaw the trial of five hundred subversives conspiring to replace papal rule with a popular party representing the proletariat's interests.

When several rebels were hanged and their bodies left swinging from the gibbet as a lesson to the rest, there was near anarchy and Rivarola's secretary was assassinated.

To divert the public's wrath away from the papacy the propaganda against the Jews was ratcheted up a notch. A long article written by the procurator general of the Dominicans, Father Ferdinand Jabalot, appeared in Rome's Ecclesiastical Journal and was then published as a pamphlet for general consumption. The Pope was so pleased that he made the author the world-wide head of the Dominicans.

It was an attempt of the most scurrilous and inflammatory kind to stir up anti-Semitic hatred accusing the Jews of all sorts of abominations: "They wash their hands in Christian blood, set fire to churches, trample the consecrated host, kidnap children and drain them of the blood and violate virgins."

Of a subtler but no less pernicious nature was the attempt to pin the blame on the Jews for the economic hardships many Christians were suffering:

"In many parts of our land the Jews have become the richest property owners. In some cities money cannot be had except through them, and so great has the number of mortgages they hold over Christians become, that it is only barely that the Christians have not yet become their vassals. Woe to us if we close our eyes! The Jews' domination will be hard, inflexible, tyrannical…"

The restrictions on Jewish freedom of movement, which had been allowed to wane, were reinforced and in 1825 the Jews in the Papal States were once again enclosed inside the ghettos. If they needed to travel for commercial reasons they had to apply for a licence from the Criminal Tribunal and upon arriving at their destination they had to show it to the local inquisitor. Warehouses and stores which had been opened up outside the ghettos had to relocate and since there was no room for them inside they were effectively closed for good.

As the Jews were not allowed to practice a profession, nor own real estate, they had to earn their living through trade as the restriction on movement was especially punitive. This also hurt the Christians who did business with them. The archbishop of Senigaglia for example complained that the annual trade fair was being severely undermined by the inquisitors' punitive measures against the Jewish businessmen who had always attended.

In Foligno a prominent Jewish family had founded a textiles factory, which employed many of the poorest townsfolk but since this went against the Church's policy of Jews employing Christians, especially Christian women, the factory had to close.

The Insignia of Gregory XVI

These and other instances of the Church's hardline stance having a direct bearing on the economic hardships experienced by the citizens of the Papal States led to a state of near-anarchy and in 1830, only two days after Mauro Cappellari, a sixty-five year-old monk, succeeded to the Throne of Peter as Gregory XVI, Bologna was in open revolt. The papal legate was run out of town and the papal banner was torn down from government buildings and replaced with the tricolore i.e. flag. Other cities followed suit and only the intervention of the Austrian army prevented the complete overthrow of the papacy.

However the moment the troops were recalled, the Papal States rose up and once again the pontiff had to appeal to Austria. For the next seven years the situation was deemed so precarious that the Austrian Army was to all intents and purposes an army of occupation.

Gregory XVI's response was to lash out at those he thought responsible for the declining influence of the Church.

"Wickedness is exultant," he declared in his encyclical Mirari Vos of 1832. "Shameless science exults. Licentiousness exults. Errors of all kinds are spread without restraint. Wicked men attack the divine authority of the Church."

He urged a return to the days when the spiritual and temporal authority of the Church was accepted without question by the common man and he reserved particular scorn for the freedom of the press, "a hateful freedom, impossible to execrate enough" which he believed responsible for spreading the notion of the separation of Church and State.

He also issued an edict reaffirming the 1775 edict of Pius VI, imposing strict regulations on the movements and livelihoods of the Jews, which he felt had been allowed to slip while his attention was focussed elsewhere.

But times had changed. All over Europe Jews were gaining new rights and these draconian measures which would once have been accepted without question, were increasingly seen as an embarrassing anachronism.

The Pope's popularity plummeted to an all-time low. His suitability for the job was called into question. In an increasingly cosmopolitan era dependent on diplomacy he was extremely parochial, speaking only Italian and spending most of his life in Venice and Rome.

A pamphlet written by a former friar was published denouncing the Church's anti-Semitic stance:

"I happen to know intimately about the task that a certain Pope Della Genga gave to a certain friar Jabalot in Rome in the year of the Jubilee [1825] to write all the worst he could think of against the Jews. And, given his ambition of being made a cardinal, he marshalled all his ingenuity not to discover, but to imagine the darkest accusations to hurl against this poor people. Then, subsidized by that same Pope Leo, he had the book printed, and distributed it for free even to those who did not want a copy."

Attacking the papal ban on Christian wetnurses attending Jewish mothers he asked:

"And if some Jewish children die for lack of nourishment, you could care less. Having to hate these people as much as possible, it only makes sense to deny milk to their children," which "seemed to contain the idea of the extermination of the race, rather than trying to bring about respect for others' beliefs or the reconciliation of Jews and Christians."

This public humiliation from within the ranks of the Roman Church was followed by a letter of complaint regarding the treatment of the Jews in the Papal States from Prince Metternich, the Austrian foreign minister, without whose troops papal rule would have crumbled at the first popular uprising.

Prince Metternich

Metternich himself had been asked to intervene by Baron Salomon Rothschild, whose government loans bankrolled the Austrian Empire. Rothschild took a personal interest in their plight and as he was from one of the most

Baron Salomon Rothschild

influential Jewish families in Europe, the request could not be treated lightly. Indeed the Vatican had borrowed from the Rothschild financial empire back in 1831 when it had needed money to quell the unrest.

The Pope's reply leaves little room for doubt as to the prevailing attitude of the papacy in the nineteenth century:

"The prohibitions on the Jews forbidding them from owning real estate… from living, where there is a ghetto, outside of its walls mixed in and confused with Christians are prohibitions founded in the sacred Canons. These, in order to guarantee Christian religion and morality, command the separation of Christians and Jews.

"Aside from the fact" he went on to say "that the Jews are forbidden such ownership by the sacred canons as a Nation of deicides and blasphemers of Christ, and sworn enemies of the Christian name, there is also the danger that the Jews will seduce and pervert those who rent from them or peasants who depend on them."

Not only would the Pope ignore Prince Metternich's request, he went so far as to reintroduce the custom of forced sermons, the practice of which had long since fallen into disuse. Worse still for the Jews, news was reaching Europe of the disappearance of a Capuchin monk, Father Tommaso, who had disappeared in Damascus.

The papers were full of lurid accounts of his fate. Having gone into the Jewish quarter to help vaccinate the children against smallpox he was supposedly seized by several Jews, including a rabbi, his throat slit and his blood drained and collected to "bake their Passover bread."

This was not the first instance of wholly unfounded accusations against the Jews of ritual murder. As long ago as 1256, ninety-one Jews held in the Tower of London were judged guilty of crucifying a little boy to celebrate Passover and hanged. The story of little Saint Hugh of Lincoln features in Chaucer's "The Prioress' Tale."

In the fifteenth century a cult grew up around the five year-old boy Lorenzino of Marostica, who was supposedly crucified on a tree by the Jews and drained of his blood. When the body was buried miracles were said to occur in the near vicinity and pilgrims were soon making their way to his shrine. The Cult received official Church approval in 1869 and the story was being told to school children as late as the 1960s.

While the furore surrounding the disappearance of the monk was still ongoing a book appeared on the scene purporting to be written by a Moldavian Jew who had converted to Orthodox Christianity. The author claimed to reveal for the first time the reasons why the Jews needed Christian blood. A catalogue of the most offensive and sensationalist accusations designed to whip up anti-Semitic hysteria, the book came into the hands of the Secretary of State Cardinal Lambruschini who saw its potential but knew that the Holy See could not be seen to endorse it.

The Orthodox Gospel Bible

His way round this dilemma was to send it to the bishop of Modena, just outside the Papal States, where it could be published in a newspaper and spread both outwards to the rest of Europe and back into the Papal States without appearing to originate from within the walls of the Vatican.

Such caution was necessary in the face of growing hostility in the press to the idea of Jewish involvement in the

Mehemet Ali

murder of the monk. Originally accepting the story at face value, the press began to suspect a plot to frame the Jews. It emerged that the confessions of guilt had been extracted under torture and fragments of bone which were previously thought to belong to the friar after he had been dismembered were now acknowledged to be animal bones.

Prince Metternich of Austria exerted pressure on Austrian newspapers to put a halt to the sensationalist reporting and personally requested the Viceroy of Syria, Mehemet Ali to put a stop to the torture which was so brutal that two of the suspects had already died.

Then the Austrian ambassador to the Holy See delivered a request to Cardinal Lambruschini from the Imperial Court of Austria that he make the Pope aware of the possibility that Father Tommaso had disappeared because he had incurred the wrath of an Arab Muslim who had publicly sworn a vendetta against him.

Not only was this story circulating widely amongst the Arab population but a Jew who testified that he saw the friar leave Damascus was beaten to death by the police to keep him from making any further statements.

Predictably enough, the Vatican refused to countenance the possibility that a man of the cloth would be hiding away fearing for his own safety while innocent men were punished for his murder. And so the propaganda continued.

The disappearance of every Christian in the area was put down to the Jews and translations of the Talmud were rolled out with attention drawn to passages which supposedly called on the Jews to torture and murder Christians wherever they found them.

Denouncing the Talmud was by then an established tradition within the Catholic Church. In 1242, the authorities ordered all copies be seized and burnt. In a papal edict in 1443 Pope Eugenius IV forbade its study and a century later Pope Julius declared the Talmud to be blasphemous. A huge pyre was prepared in the middle of the Campo dei Fiori and hundreds of copies confiscated from the ghetto were publicly burnt.

Once again it was the Jew's apparent need for Christian blood in their rituals that was paramount but

Campo dei Fiori

there was something else which would become increasingly important as the century wore on:

"God permits the Jews to seize the property of Christians in any way they can, by ruse, trickery, usury or theft."

When it became politically expedient for the Viceroy to appease Austria and Britain whose navy had just seized several Egyptian supply ships, he released the remaining imprisoned Jews. The Vatican trumpeted this as proof of a high-level international conspiracy of Jews and Freemasons using their nexus of financial and political contacts to stage-manage global affairs, a plan that included the destruction of the Church.

As the modern era progressed and the idea of absolute rule under a divinely ordained Pope became less and less tenable, this kind of paranoid sentiment would become entrenched in the Vatican's rhetoric as it lashed out at the perceived enemies it held responsible for its waning influence.

When Gregory XVI died in June 1846, the conclave that gathered to elect a successor may not have known it but time was running out for the Papal States. The man they elected was Giovanni Maria Mastai-Ferretti, who at only fifty-four was one of the youngest ever Popes. He had proved his worth however in leading the Church in Romagna, which had experienced violent opposition to papal rule and the cardinals thought he was the right man to steer the Vatican through the troubled times ahead.

Pius IX would introduce. News reached the Vatican that many of the elite dining clubs had voted to admit Jews in a gesture of fellowship. A pamphlet was circulated which spread the word that the Pope was about to tear down the ghetto walls. Everywhere there was an air of expectancy as the imminent reforms were awaited.

For Pius IX, who had no intention of granting equal citizenship to the Jews, this was just one of a number of pressing problems facing him as the year 1848 began. In January, the citizens of Palermo revolted and forced the King of Naples to sign a constitution. In February King Louis Philippe of France was ousted by insurgents and the following month Metternich was driven into exile.

Insurgents in the Papal States took advantage of the fact that the Austrian Army's attention was elsewhere and

King Louis Philippe of France

He was popular with the public too, for he was seen as a simple and sincere man of devout religious views who had taken no part in the intrigues which had come to dominate the Vatican in recent years. Unlike some of his predecessors who had seemed imperial and aloof from the day-to-day problems facing the citizenry, he was thought of as friendly and approachable.

It seemed that a new era of tolerance towards the Jews would be ushered in and rumors spread of the reforms rose up. Bologna fell and Rome started to topple. The papal prime minister was stabbed in the center of Rome and Pius IX fled the Holy City in the carriage of the Bavarian ambassador, disguised as a simple priest.

In December, Giuseppe Garibaldi and the nationalist leader Giuseppe Mazzini entered Rome at the head of

Giuseppe Mazzini

Giuseppe Garibaldi

a revolutionary army and declared the end of papal rule and the beginning of a Roman Republic. Once again an invading force freed the Jews from the ghetto. The Pope was outraged and from his fortress in Gaeta, in the kingdom of

Naples, called on his loyal subjects across Europe to help him regain the papal throne. By July when French forces invaded Rome, the revolution was at end and the Pope was soon back in power. But things had changed forever.

Despite agreeing to abolish the ghetto in order to secure a loan from the Rothschilds, the Pope made it clear that he wanted the rights, which the Jews had won under the 1848 statutes, to be rescinded. Tuscany quickly acceded as did the duchy of Modena but the kingdom of Sardinia allowed the statutes to remain and the Jews there were able to take advantage of their new-found freedoms, attending university classes, widening their business contacts, and printing a free press to highlight the plight of the Jews in the

Papal States living under the strictures of the Inquisition.

This was of crucial importance in the attention brought to the case of a young Jewish boy seized by the authorities in Bologna and brought to the House of Catechumens on the basis of testimony given by a servant girl who claimed to have secretly baptized him.

Pius IX showed a staggering ignorance of the changes that had taken place in the last half century by following the letter of Canon Law and acting as his predecessors had done since time immemorial. Whereas previously the only complaints to greet such action would have come from the Jews, now there were storms of protest from around the world, as news spread of the abduction of a six year-old boy from his parents. The movement for the unification of Italy, in whose way stood the Pope's claim to rule the Papal States on divine authority, made tremendous popular gains as the Pope increasingly looked like an embarrassing throwback to the Middle Ages, completely out of place in modern Europe.

It even looked at one point as though the French Government would withdraw the French troops from Rome, which were the only security against further popular uprisings.

"The Holy See's actions in this matter" wrote the French foreign minister to the ambassador in Rome "constitute a violation of the most basic guarantees that involve respect for the domestic family and for paternal authority. You would do well, Duke, to let the secretary of state know how much pain the Holy See is causing the Emperor's Government. You should tell him that public sentiment has been profoundly wounded in learning that Monsieur Mortar has tried in vain to reclaim his son from the Papal Government. The feeling of unpleasant surprise felt by the faithful was only equalled by the joy it has given the enemies of Catholicism."

When it became clear that the Pope would not relent despite the building international pressure the ambassador wrote back:

"The proprieties of the current century, the riling of public opinion fade before these celestial prescriptions and the Pope, fortified in his belief, demonstrates the unshakeable firmness that he adopts on certain occasions. In the century in which we live this tendency can become the source of major complications and serious dangers, especially when it is combined, as in Pius IX's case, with a lively and at times impetuous nature."

In the Pope's mind there was a very simple solution to the problem and this involved the parents converting to Christianity, in which case he was only too willing to reunite them with their son. To his blinkered way of thinking he simply could not understand why anyone should wish to refuse the blessings of the Holy Spirit.

But this intransigent stance which had been the Pope's prerogative for over a thousand years was no longer tenable in an increasingly secular society and it would lead to his undoing.

His position in regard to the Jewish boy and his unwillingness to get behind the movement for Italian independence from Austria because of his duty as spiritual father to all the faithful played into the hands of the champions for unification and within a year they had run the papal forces out of Bologna and swept through the rest of the Papal States, supported by the French troops.

Romagna was annexed, then the Marches, followed by Umbria. As a sign of the new times ahead, the Inquisitor in Bologna who had ordered the arrest of the boy was taken from his Dominican monastery and thrown into jail, charged with abduction.

For the time being the security of Rome and the Roman Campagna was guaranteed by Napoleon III's forces

Napoleon III

although tested by Garibaldi's troops in 1862 and again in 1867. But when the Franco-German war broke out in 1870, the garrison was withdrawn. With only a token force left

to defend the city, General Raffaele Cadorna stormed the Porta Pia on September 20th. The new secular kingdom of Italy had a capital and the Pope had to content himself with the Vatican.

Over the course of the previous decade as time was running out for the Papal States, a sense of desperation and paranoia could be sensed in the Vatican's treatment of the Jews. Because they were the most conspicuous beneficiaries of the modernizing movement, it was a short step to viewing them as the driving force behind it.

There was already a centuries-old distrust of the Jews, nurtured by the Church which never missed an opportunity to remind the faithful that they were the arch-enemies of Christ bent on an eternal attempt to recreate the killing of the Messiah by torturing and murdering as many Christians as they could lay their hands on.

But from this time onwards there is a discernible trend in the Vatican's reaction to events, which seeks to discredit the forces for social change, such as democracy and the free press, by painting it as a Judaic conspiracy to take over the world.

In Pius IX's encyclical *Quanta Cura*, he set forth his Syllabus of Errors, highlighting no less than eighty ways in which the modern world was leading the faithful from the path. Chief among them were the separation of Church and State, freedom of religion and the removal of education from the hands of the clergy.

Never one to mince his words he warned:"In these times the haters of truth and justice and the most bitter enemies of our religion deceive the people and lie maliciously. They disseminate impious doctrines by means of pestilential books, pamphlets, and newspapers distributed over the whole world. Nor are you ignorant of the fact that in our age some men are found who, moved by the spirit of Satan, have sunk to that degree of impiety in which they do not shrink from denying our Ruler and Lord Jesus Christ, or from impugning His Divinity with wicked pertinacity."

It is at this point that those behind the "war being waged against the Catholic Church" are explicitly identified as an unholy alliance of Jews and Freemasons.

Giuseppe Garibaldi, who twice tried to storm Rome, made no secret of his membership of the Masonic Brotherhood, but that is not what the Pope is alluding to.

When Freemasonry declared itself in 1717, it became apparent that virtually every member of the Royal Society of London for the Improvement of Natural Knowledge, known today simply as the Royal Society, was a Freemason.

The Royal Society itself had its roots in an "Invisible College" in which men of science from London, Oxford and Cambridge could meet in secret to discuss their research unmolested by the Church. This was shortly after Galileo Galilei was forced to renounce his astronomical discoveries to obtain release from the papal prisons.

Learned men who wanted to pursue their studies but did not necessarily want to renounce their faith because of what they saw as a Church temporarily led astray would have embraced the principles of Freemasonry. One of its most central tenets stipulates that it does not matter what religion you practice so long as you believe in a Supreme Being.

For the same reason, Jews would have been welcomed into Masonic lodges at a time when all over Europe they were denied entry into dining clubs. The relief at being able to socialize with one's business peers without constantly being reminded that one was responsible for the death of the

Galileo Galilei

Messiah can be readily imagined. Furthermore the emphasis on Old Testament imagery such as the building of Solomon's Temple would have made Freemasonry attractive, as would the principle of self-improvement through education to a class of people denied places at schools and universities.

The very idea that all faiths were equally valid, their various deities simply manifestations of one ultimate divine source, was anathema to the Catholic Church, which

Solomon's Temple

believed it was the one true faith, with the divine right to seek the suppression of all other religions because they were mere superstitions.

"Anyone who knows the nature, desires and intentions of the sects" wrote Pius IX "cannot doubt that the present misfortune must mainly be imputed to the frauds and machinations of these sects."

The explicit connection to the Jews can be readily seen in his use of the term "the synagogue of Satan, which gathers its troops against the Church of Christ."

When a book entitled "The Jew: Judaism and the Judaization of Christian peoples" appeared in 1869 reiterating the Jewish need for Christian blood and the commandments in the Talmud "to cheat and kill the Christian whenever he finds an occasion to do so" Pius IX awarded the author the Cross of Commander of the Papal Order.

While the Italian government's troops made a futile attempt to reach an agreement with the Pope, which would allow him to play an active role in the hand over of Rome rather than having it seized by force, Pius IX was more concerned with the proclamation of papal infallibility as official Church doctrine at the First Vatican Council.

When the troops were ordered in, the Pope confined himself to the Vatican palaces and although he had complete freedom of movement he portrayed himself as a prisoner of the Italian Government. For the next fifty-eight years no pope would venture outside the walls of the Vatican and indeed the Italian State only received official papal recognition in 1929 with the signing of the Concordat with Mussolini.

Convinced he was under siege from the evil forces of modernism the rhetoric against the perceived Jewish-Masonic conspiracy bordered on the hysterical. He found confirmation of it wherever he looked. What had allowed the Italian forces to seize Rome? The withdrawal of the garrison to fight the Franco-Prussian war. Who had bankrolled the French forces? The Jewish banker Alphonse de Rothschild. And who had bankrolled Bismarck? The Jewish banker Gerson Bleichroder.

Because the Jews had been traditionally denied the right to own real estate and practice professions, they had earned money through trade and banking. As a consequence of specialization in these economic activities, several Jews had become immensely wealthy and powerful. Naturally, they had invested in the emergent industries, among them the press. With spreading literacy, advances in printing technology which made it financially viable and the newly won freedom of the press, this was undoubtedly a very sound speculation for investors.

The Pope however saw it differently. For him, this was proof that the Jewish-Masonic conspiracy was not only behind the attacks in the press on the powers of the Church, it was using this new medium to poison vulnerable young minds against their spiritual father, God's chosen representative on earth.

Such thinking has a very ancient pedigree. As far back as the fourteenth century Jews were blamed for spreading the Black Death by poisoning wells in a concerted

Black Death

attempt to destroy European Christian civilization. But in that instance the Popes came to their defence, calling for the attacks on the Jewish population to cease.

Whereas previous papal outbursts had focussed on the supposed religious duties of the Jews to conspire against Christians, the new perceived threat was from freethinking Jewish atheists who espoused the new social doctrine of "egalité, liberté et fraternité" which the French Revolution had introduced to Europe.

This was in part a way of dealing with the thorny problem that Jesus had been born a Jew, as had the founding fathers of the Christian Church and the Old Testament, although second in prominence to the Gospels was a sacred Christian text, which had both given Christian society its laws and prophesied the birth of Christ.

Thus a distinction was drawn between the Jews in their state of innocence before the rejection and murder of Christ and the Jews in their fallen state ever since.

An Image from the Gospels

The rapid rise in status of many Jews, most of whom only half a century earlier were confined to the ghetto and forbidden from owning real estate or practicing a profession fell right into the hands of those who sought to traduce their reputation. The rational explanation that it was the result of hard work and the fortuitous exploitation of new opportunities in expanding industries was cast aside. Instead it was painted as a sinister spreading nexus of influence, financed by the gold of the elite Jewish bankers, which had become the golden calf to which the Israelites turned in the desert in disobedience to Jehovah's will. The ultimate aim was nothing less than global domination and the forces of Liberalism and Socialism in particular were its weapons with which it sought the destruction of the principle obstacle in its path, namely the Catholic Church.

The Insignia of Leo XIII

As Pope Leo XIII made abundantly clear in his encyclical Humanum Genus issued in 1884, the Catholic Church was opposed to democracy. What it wanted was a return to the old style of government, namely a populace that was absolutely obedient to an autocratic ruler, who ruled with the sanction of the Church. This was the classic relationship of Church and Crown. The idea that people should elect their government, which in effect served rather than ruled the people without any input from the Church was anathema.

When Leo XIII made this statement he was the first Pope in hundreds of years who, because of the loss of the Papal States, was only a priest and not also a king.

All around the world the influence of the Catholic Church was on the wane. The revolution in Mexico led by Benito Juarez resulted in the loss of Church lands and revenue. As well as outlawing monasteries and convents the new governments had put a stop to the practice of sending Church funds back to Rome. The Pope was told in no uncertain terms that the role of the Church was the pastoral care of its spiritual children, not the generation of wealth. The same thing had happened when Latin America was liberated from Spanish rule by Simon Bolivar and Jose de San Martin.

The fact that both Simon Bolivar and Benito Juarez, the first Indian president of Mexico, were Freemasons, as were virtually all the signers of the American Declaration of Independence, which had thrown off the yoke of Imperial rule and guaranteed freedom of worship, confirmed the Pope in his view that the Church was under siege. The rumors abounding that the French Revolution was orchestrated by Freemasons can only have made his position more entrenched.

"The principles of social science follow" he complains. "Here naturalists teach that men have all the same rights, and are perfectly equal in condition; that every man is naturally independent; that no one has a right to command others; that it is tyranny to keep men subject to any other authority than that which emanates from themselves. Hence the people are sovereign; those who rule have no authority but by the commission and concession of the people; so that they can be deposed, willing or unwilling, according to the wishes of the people. The origin of all rights and civil duties is in the people or in the state, which

Benito Juarez

San Martín proclaiming the independence of Peru

is ruled according to the new principles of liberty. The State must be godless; no reason why one religion ought to be preferred to another; all to be held in the same esteem.

"Now it is well-known that Freemasons approve these maxims, and that they wish to see governments shaped on this pattern and model needs no demonstration."

From his papal throne in the Vatican palace under siege from all sides, he writes as though he is seeing the kingdom of Satan springing up before his very eyes. Indeed he was so mistrustful that he slept with all the Vatican gold under his bed!

However to a modern mind in the 21st century his words are no more than the description of the democratic values their forefathers fought for, and they have come to expect as their birthright.

The world was simply changing too fast for an essentially conservative institution, with a vested interest in maintaining the status quo.

The socialist movement was gathering pace, with a growing proletariat that had established its First International in 1864. Their calls for the abolition of private property disturbed the European aristocracy as much as it did the Church.

The illiterate masses were learning to read, and asking awkward questions. Whereas once they would have

Karl Marx

sought guidance and a sense of community in the local parish church, they now belonged to socialist-dominated trade unions, where they were introduced to ideas of social justice they would never have heard from the priest.

The Catholic Church must have felt as hard-pressed in the nineteenth century as it had ever been, with the possible exception of the early years of Roman persecution. Despite its constant assertion that it was under attack from enemies on all sides, it does not take the benefit of hindsight to see that it was its own worst enemy. Lashing out at the perceived Judaic-Masonic conspiracy only served to make it look increasingly out of touch.

It is intriguing to ponder what lessons were learnt as it went on to face an even harder time in the twentieth century, with the problems of Communism, Fascism, global warfare, and growing agnosticism, let alone the questions and dilemmas thrown up by the advances in genetic research.

chapter 8

ONE OF THE BIGGEST SCANDALS TO HIT THE VATICAN OCCURRED AS A RESULT OF THE INFILTRATION OF THE HIGHEST ECHELONS OF THE CATHOLIC CHURCH BY AN ITALIAN MASONIC LODGE KNOWN AS P2, THE ABBREVIATION OF PROPAGANDA DUE. SO FAR-REACHING WERE ITS IMPLICATIONS THAT IT BROUGHT DOWN THE COALITION GOVERNMENT UNDER ARNALDO FORLANI AND WAS EVEN HELD TO BE LINKED TO THE DEATH OF POPE JOHN PAUL I.

P2 and the

Pope Paul VI

The controversy centers on four men: Licio Gelli, Michele Sindona, Bishop Paul Marcinkus and Roberto Calvi. P2 was the glue that joined together their unholy alliance. Formed by Giordano Gamberini in 1966 with the stated aim of establishing a nexus of powerful men who could further the cause of Freemasonry, P2 took its name from a lodge that was inaugurated by the Grand Orient of Italy in Turin over a century earlier.

It rapidly established itself as pre-eminent in the country, including many nobles and even royalty among its brethren, but when Licio Gelli rose to the level of Master Mason, the current Italian Grand Orient was so concerned at the direction his activities were taking the lodge that he officially severed all ties and publicly disowned it.

A prominent businessman and manufacturer, Licio Gelli had cut his teeth fighting alongside the fascists in the Spanish Civil War in the Italian Blackshirt Division and during World War II, he had been a liaison officer with the Nazis, rising to the rank of Oberleutenant in the S.S. After the war, he faced a war crimes trial accused of murdering and torturing patriots, but he had worked for both sides, and Communist allies made sure that the case against him collapsed.

For a while, he was involved with arranging "ratlines" to help Nazis fleeing justice escape to South America. When this was no longer lucrative, he went to Argentina and aligned himself first with General Peron and then with the right-wing junta that ousted him. When General Peron later returned to exile from power, several witnesses confirmed that he kneeled in gratitude before Gelli.

Whenever a new member joined P2, he was obliged to show his loyalty by bringing with him information that would compromise not only himself, but others in his professional or political sphere. Gelli then had a hold on the new member and when he threatened the contacts with blackmail, he invariably gained yet more initiates and more contacts and so the web was spun ever wider.

Another cunning ruse was to find out the shortlists of candidates for promotion to the very top positions in industry and finance, call each one and tell him that he intended to use his influence to secure the job for him. Then all he had to do was sit back and wait for the successful candidate to join his lodge in gratitude.

Vatican Bank

The Freemasons had been proscribed under Mussolini but they were rehabilitated under the post-war Democratic Government and Licio Gelli saw a great opportunity to exploit this new source of power and influence. Totally disregarding the essential principles of Freemasonry as a tool for psychological and moral self-improvement, he targeted retired senior members of the Armed Forces and through them he gained introductions to active service heads of staff. He was a past master in the art of corruption and knew fully well that the way to power lay through knowledge.

As the Venerable Master of the Lodge, Gelli was the only one who knew the full extent of the circle of influence he had consolidated. P2 was divided into seventeen cells, each with its own group leader and these group leaders only knew the membership of their own cell.

By the 1970s, his infiltration of Italian aristocratic, administrative, executive, judicial, financial and military establishments was complete and Italy appeared to be well and truly rotten to the core.

Among the men who had sworn an oath of allegiance to him were: the Commander of the Armed Forces, and

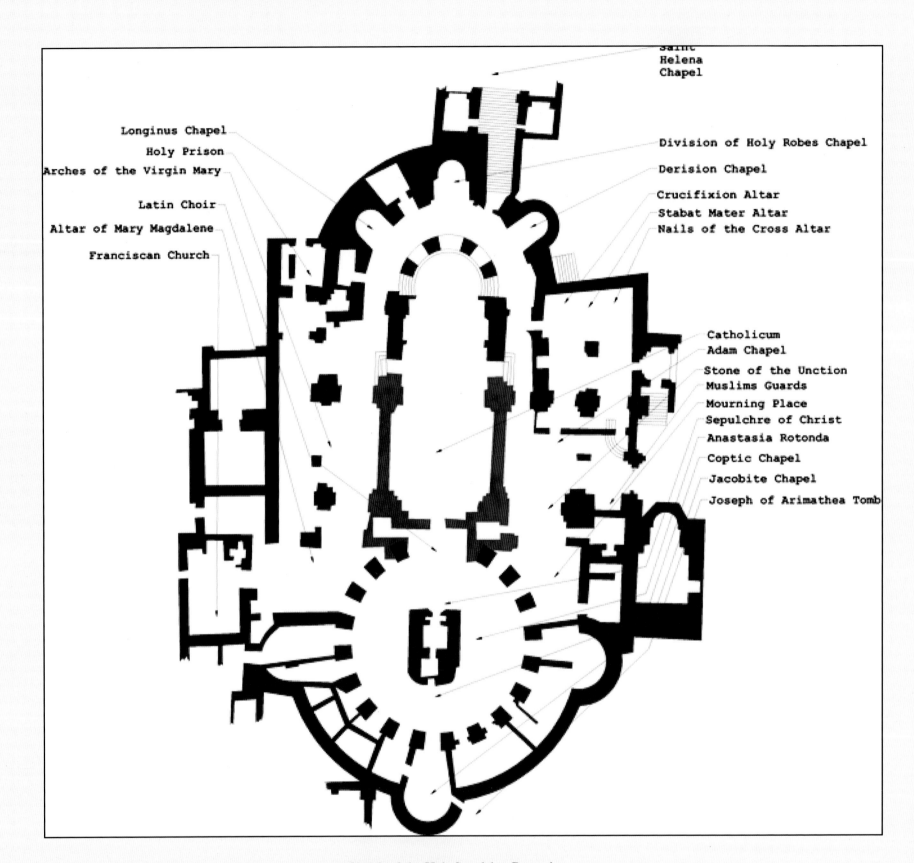

Longinus Chapel
Holy Prison
Arches of the Virgin Mary

Latin Choir
Altar of Mary Magdalene

Franciscan Church

Saint
Helena
Chapel

Division of Holy Robes Chapel

Derision Chapel

Crucifixion Altar
Stabat Mater Altar
Nails of the Cross Altar

Catholicum
Adam Chapel
Stone of the Unction
Muslims Guards
Mourning Place
Sepulchre of Christ
Anastasia Rotonda
Coptic Chapel
Jacobite Chapel
Joseph of Arimathea Tomb

Sketch of the Holy Sepulcher Rotonda

seven other admirals, thirty generals and three heads of the secret service (the Defence Chief of Staff, the Chief of Military Counter-Espionage and the Chief of National Security), the head of Italy's Financial Police, the editor of Il Corriere della Sera, the leading newspaper, top industrialists and bankers, nineteen judges, cabinet ministers and politicians from every party except the Communist Party.

It has since become apparent that the goal of P2 was a secret right-wing power base which would control the country from behind the scenes, unless the Communists came to power in which case they would use the army to arrange a coup d'etat.

It is not clear who was Gelli's main point of entry into the otherwise almost hermetically sealed world of the Vatican. Despite the papal pronouncement that membership of Freemasonry was not only incompatible with the Catholic faith but it would actually result in excommunication, there were several prominent officials within the Vatican who were members of P2.

Gelli probably infiltrated the Vatican through one of his most useful P2 brethren, Umberto Ortolani, who was known as "the Puppet Master." A successful businessman and lawyer, he had links with the Vatican that went back as far as the 1950s. Indeed he was so close to Cardinal

World War II

Lercaro that people thought, and Ortolani did not correct them, that they were cousins.

During the run-up to the election of Pope Paul VI, Ortolani offered his villa as a venue for a meeting attended by a faction who wanted to ensure the election of their candidate and when they were successful, Ortolani was granted the Vatican award of "Gentleman of his Holiness" in gratitude.

He was subsequently able to get Gelli affiliated to the Knights of Malta and the Holy Sepulcher, the order descended from the Knights Hospitallers, which is recognized as a sovereign state by the Vatican. This was all the more remarkable because Gelli was not even a practicing Catholic.

Some prominent church officials may have believed that the Vatican and P2 had a common cause in their fear and loathing of Communism. Gelli's favorite phrase was a quote by cardinal Hinsley of Westminster who said in 1935: "If Fascism goes under, God's cause goes under with it."

In the late 1960s, Michele Sindona joined P2. Known as the "Shark" by his friends in recognition of his shrewd financial wheeling and dealing, he had close links with both the Sicilian Mafia and the five New York Cosa Nostra families Colombo, Bonanno, Lucchese, Genovese and in particular the Gambinos. He used his financial acumen to launder Mafia money earned dealing in drugs, prostitution, gambling, protection and racketeering.

Born in Sicily, he earned his stripes on the Black Market during World War II. Accounting and tax law soon became his speciality, skills which were indispensable to the cash-rich Mafia and he was able to invest their money and move it in and out of Italy without accruing any tax burdens.

With Mafia money, he began to buy banks and set up holding companies as a slick way to transfer funds out of the country. Realizing the potential goldmine that the Vatican represented, he curried favor with the Archbishop of Milan by putting up over two million dollars (of Mafia money!) for an old people's home, and soon the diocese was relying almost exclusively upon him for financial advice.

He paid particular care to cultivate the friendships of the Administrative Secretary of the Vatican Bank and Monsignor Sergio Guerri, the man in charge of the Special Administration, which looked after the Vatican investments around the world.

The third man in this quartet of fraud, Roberto Calvi, was known variously in Masonic circles as the "Knight" and the "Paymaster" in recognition of his huge financial clout. When the corruption scandal was eventually exposed to the glare of public scrutiny, journalists dubbed him "God's Banker" because of the web of deceit that connected him to the Vatican Bank.

The fourth and final player, Bishop Paul Marcinkus, grew up on the mean streets of mob-run Cicero, Illinois, in the twenties and thirties when Al Capone had moved his empire of speak-easies and gambling dens there. The son of poor Lithuanian immigrants, he saw the priesthood as a way of escaping the grinding poverty into which he had been born and he progressed

Archdiocese of Chicago

quickly through the ranks. He soon impressed the Head of the Archdiocese of Chicago, who recommended him for a post in the English Section of the Vatican Secretary of State's office in 1952.

Al Capone

It was there that he caught the eye of Pope Paul in 1964 during a visit to downtown Rome. The crowd surged forward to greet the pontiff and he might have been crushed, had not Marcinkus used his 6 ft 3 ins. and 16 - stone frame to shield him. Driving a path through the press of bodies, he brought the pope to safety and thereafter became his unofficial bodyguard, earning the nickname "The Gorilla." When the Prefecture of the Economic Affairs of the Holy See was created in 1967, to audit the Vatican wealth, Marcinkus was promoted to Bishop and made the Secretary of the Vatican Bank, despite protesting that he had no banking experience!

The modern source of the Vatican wealth goes back to a payment made by Mussolini to the Vatican under the terms of the Lateran agreement in 1929. In exchange for Vatican support, Mussolini agreed to guarantee religious teaching in schools and not to pass laws, which would contravene the tenets of the Catholic faith. In addition, he citizens and exemption from paying taxes on its holdings and duties on imported goods.

The Special Administration was created by Pope Pius XI to manage this windfall with Bernardino Nogara given free rein to invest the money as he saw fit, a situation that led to the Church breaking its own ban on usury and even owning shares in a pharmaceutical company that manufactures a contraceptive!

Nogara was a very shrewd investor, and soon enough, the Vatican was seeing a nice return on its money. He bought shares in Italgas, which had a virtual monopoly on the supply of gas to urban centers in Italy, and placed the brother of the next pope, Francesco Pacelli, on the board of directors. In a display of nepotism not seen since the day of the Borgias, three of the pope's nephews were soon on the board of a host of companies up and down the country.

Before World War II, Nogara used many of the assets to buy gold, making an original purchase of $26.8 million at $35 per ounce and more than doubling his money when he sold $5 million on the free market. He also acquired controlling interests in a plethora of banks and utilities companies, investing in water, electricity, the railroad network, telecommunications, and was even able to repay Mussolini's generosity by selling him munitions from an arms factory he had purchased on behalf of the Vatican when Mussolini invaded Ethiopia.

Italian Coins

Emblem of Boniface IV

undertook to pay the "the sum of 750 million lire and to hand over at the same time Consolidated 5 per cent State Bonds to the bearer for the nominal value of one billion lire."

Crucially, the Vatican was recognized as a separate sovereign state, complete with diplomatic immunity for its

Hitler in Wien

had moved into insurance, real estate, cement, steel, finance, flour and even spaghetti! Vatican financial partners included Rothschilds of Paris and London, Hambros, Morgan Guarantee, The Bankers Trust Company of New York, Credit Suisse and Chase Manhattan. Through his purchase of 15% of the Italian construction company Societa Generale Immobiliare, the Vatican acquired an incredible list of properties around the world, that included the Stock Exchange Tower in Montreal, a 277 acre residential area in Oyster Bay, New York, and even an entire satellite city of Mexico City, making the Vatican the biggest owner of private real estate in the world.

In 1942, while Mussolini was preoccupied with the war, Nogara was once again devoting his energies to increasing the Vatican wealth. By examining certain clauses of the original Lateran Treaty, he established that the Italian Government had forfeited its right to tax ecclesiastical corporations under the Holy See and he got the then Director General of the Finance Ministry to agree that neither the Vatican Bank nor the Special Administration should pay tax on share dividends.

It is estimated that Nogara transformed that original gift from Mussolini into $500 million to be overseen by the Special Administration, $650 million controlled by the Ordinary Section of the APSA (the Administration of the Patrimony of the Holy See), and assets in the Vatican Bank worth over $940 million.

The Administration of Religious Works had been created in 1887 by Pope Pius XII to administer money for charitable causes. In 1942, its name was changed to the Institute for Religious Works (I.O.R.) and it was soon known unofficially as the Vatican Bank.

By the time Nogara retired in 1954, he had purchased shares on behalf of the Vatican in: T.W.A, General Electric, Shell, Gulf Oil, General Motors, and I.B.M. He

The Italian Government looked with envy on this huge untapped resource of potential revenue, and in 1962, legislation was passed to tax these share dividends. Naturally, it was hampered in its efforts as the Vatican retained its official status as a sovereign state and any negotiations had to take place through diplomatic channels with ambassadors having to seek an audience with their respective counterparts.

The Vatican was adamant that by the terms of the original agreement, it should be granted tax exemption for both its banks, the I.O.R and the

Pope Pius XII

Special Administration, but in the coalition government of Christian Democrats and Socialists, the Finance minister was a socialist who was not about to kowtow.

Faced with the scandal of his resignation in protest, the Prime Minister asked as a compromise that the Vatican at least provide a list of all its major share-holdings. But the Vatican refused, and in 1964, the situation became so fraught that Church officials at one stage threatened to flood the market, already in serious decline, with their entire holdings which would have ruined the Italian economy.

The Government of the day had no choice but to drop the matter but questions were asked in the press. Articles condemning the materialism of the Vatican started to appear, such as the following in Il Mondo:

"Is it right for the Vatican to operate in markets like a speculator? Is it right for the Vatican to have a bank whose operations help the illegal transfer of capital from Italy to other countries? Is it right for that bank to assist Italians in evading tax?

"The Church preaches equality, but it does not seem to us that the best way to ensure equality is by evading taxes, which constitute the means by which the Lay State tries to promote the same equality."

And so, in response to the growing calls for the Church to return to the simplicity and material poverty that was so central to the teachings of Christ, and with the threat that finally came in 1968 that by the end of the year the Vatican would have to start paying up, the decision was taken to sell its huge share portfolio, which by then had become the source of much embarrassing investigative journalism.

The plan was for the Vatican to transfer its investments in the Italian financial markets to foreign markets, and begin to invest in Eurodollar blue-chips and off-shore

Prime Minister - Aldo Moro Haly

Dr. Luigi Mennini

Sindona offered to take a large part of the portfolio including the shares in Societa Gerneral Immobiliare, which had assets worth over half a billion dollars. The shares were paid for, with money illegally converted from deposits at a bank he had acquired called Banca Privata Finanziaria and the deal was arranged by Umberto Ortolani, Licio Gelli's right hand man.

He also purchased a controlling stake in Finabank, the Banque de Financement in Geneva, which still left the Vatican with 29% of the shares. Hambros of London were so impressed that they bought shares in Banca Privata as did the Continental Bank of Illinois, which handled the majority of the Vatican's investment in America.

Slowly, Sindona was spinning his web around the Vatican and pretty soon, it would discover that it was stuck fast no matter how it struggled to get free.

From sworn affidavits of employees at the banks when the scandal broke, it is apparent that these banks were being used to disguise financial fraud on a huge scale. Money was stolen from the accounts of depositors, moved to an account held by the Vatican Bank and then moved again to another account at Finabank in Switzerland, minus a 15% commission of course. Here, the money was used to speculate on the financial markets and the losses (which by the time the Swiss bank inspectors put a stop to it amounted to over $30 million) were financed by a shell company called Liberfinco (Liberian Financial Company.)

Another bank, which Sindona took off the hands of the Vatican, while still leaving it with part-ownership, was the Banca Unione. Under his guidance, it seemed to be doing particularly well, with its deposits rising from $35 million to $150 million whereas in reality, yet another robbery was being staged behind the scenes, and in total, $250 million

profits. Unfortunately, this is how they became involved with the Shark.

Sindona had already made himself indispensable to Massimo Spada, the Administrative Secretary of the Vatican Bank and Board member of many of the companies owned on behalf of the Vatican. He also targeted Luigi Mennini, another top Vatican official, but his shrewdest move was undoubtedly to cultivate the close friendship of Monsignor Sergio Guerri, who was running the Special Administration.

was siphoned off into the Amincor Bank of Zuric, yes you guessed it also owned by Sindona!!

Soon enough, the illegal transfer of money out of Italy was beginning to effect the Lira and when Sindona began to manipulate the Milan Stock Market with Roberto Calvi, such was the effect on the economy that unemployment levels and the cost of living began to increase. One single illegal kick-back given by Sindona to Calvi and Bishop Marcinkus for buying shares that had been artificially elevated was said to have been as much $6.5 million at 1972 levels of inflation.

Calvi had begun his financial career working for the Banco Ambrosiano in Milan, known as the Priest's Bank because a written deposition guaranteeing one's faith was required before one could use its services. The Archbishop of Milan banked there and board meetings were begun with prayers.

Pope John Paul I

Calvi set his sights on the Banca Cattolica del Veneto, which had been used by Albino Luciani, Pope John Paul I. Traditionally, it had loaned money to clergy at good rates for the purpose of charitable works. Calvi acquired the option to buy it from Marcinkus, hoping to trade on the good name it had by its association with men of the cloth.

Predictably enough, the low interest rates stopped when Calvi took over and when complaints were made it was discovered that Marcinkus had sold 37% of the controlling 51% held by the I.O.R which was meant to guarantee against a takeover by a third party. Not only this, but Marcinkus had helped conceal from the Bank of Italy the illegal activities Calvi had undertaken by putting at his disposal, the facilities of the Vatican Bank. According to Under Secretary of State Monsignor Benelli, the shares were sold at an artificially low price and the mark-up of 31 billion lire paid to Marcinkus as a sweetener.

Meanwhile, further evidence was accruing of Marcinkus' unsuitability for the post of President of the Vatican Bank. In April 1973, William Lynch, Chief of the Organized Crime and Racketeering Office of the U.S. Department of Justice and the Assistant Chief of the Strike Force in the Southern District of New York, accompanied by two officials from the FBI, came to the Vatican to pursue their investigation into the forgery of $14.5 million of counterfeit bonds.

They claimed to have incontrovertible proof that "someone with financial authority" within the Vatican Bank had ordered the bonds as a down payment of an eventual $950 million. Trial deposits had been made at the Handelsbank in Zurich and the Banco di Roma, and would have been passed off as genuine had not the banks sent samples to the Bankers Association in New York.

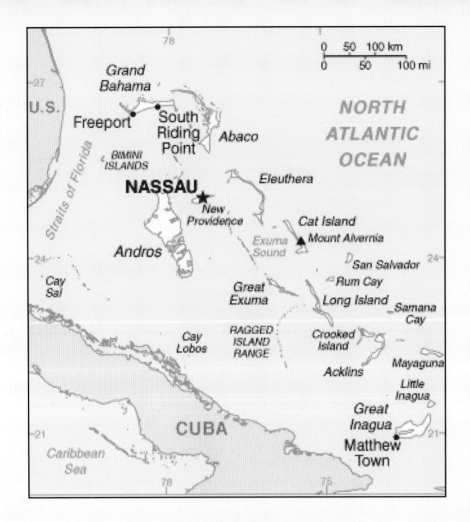

According to Mario Foligni, who cut a deal when he was arrested, the bonds were destined to be used by Marcinkus and Sindona to purchase the Italian giant Bastogi. Foligni also testified that Sindona had opened a series of private numbered accounts for Marcinkus in the Bahamas. Although Marcinkus denied the existence of these accounts to the American investigators who questioned him, he was certainly on the board of directors of Banco Ambrosiano Overseas in Nassau, the capital of the Bahamas. Sindona and Calvi had persuaded him to accept the position with a gift of 2.5% of the stock so they could use the Vatican name.

The Mafia began using Finabank to clean money on its way into Italy, and as Sindona cleverly ensured that the distinctions between his own financial interests and that of the Vatican's were so blurred, often by persuading the Vatican to retain a portion of the shares he was sold, soon

enough the Vatican Bank was hopelessly mixed up in the international "laundry" business.

Meanwhile, Sindona turned his attention to America and after purchasing the Franklin National Bank of New York, the twentieth largest bank in America, he tried to gain a foothold in the corridors of power of the world's largest economy by offering Richard Nixon's Presidential Campaign Chief Fund Raiser a suitcase containing a million dollars cash, "to show his faith in America."

Richard Nixon

Before long however, the chickens were coming home to roost for the man that the Italian Prime Minister had once described as "The savior of the Lira". At the beginning of 1974, the stock market went into decline and "Il Crack Sindona" as the Italian newspapers dubbed it, began to appear.

He had been using his banks to siphon off money for such a long time that a huge hole began to appear, which he could no longer cover up. The U.S. Government was so alarmed at the prospect of the collapse of the Franklin Bank that they gave it unlimited access to the Federal Reserve. In Italy, his Banca Privata was propped up with $128 million dollars, but to no avail. In October of the same years, both the Franklin and the Privata banks collapsed, costing the Federal Reserve Insurance Corporation over $2 billion, the worst disaster in American banking history. By comparison, the Vatican got off lightly, losing an estimated $27 million plus their shares in Banca Privata. When Finabank followed suit, the losses were a good deal higher, at anything up to $240 million.

It was now that Sindona's Masonic connections paid off, for corrupt sources in the judiciary and the police force tipped off Gelli that Sindona was about to be arrested and he was able to flee the country.

When questioned about his relationship with Sindona, Marcinkus told L'Espresso "The truth is that I

Prime Minister Pope Mariano Rumors

don't even know him. How can I have lost money because of him. The Vatican has not lost a cent, the rest is pure fantasy."

The Secretary Inspector of the Vatican Bank, Dr. Luigi Mennini, had his passport confiscated after "Il Crack Sindona," but strenuously denied involvement with Sindona. However, Carlo Bordoni who turned state's evidence attested that, "He was a seasoned gambler... He speculated in Finabank, in shares, in commodities. He was a virtual slave to Sindona's blackmail. Sindona had often threatened to make public information, Mennini's illegal operations carried out with Finabank."

While Sindona was fighting extradition in America, Roberto Calvi took over the business of speculating on behalf of Vatican Incorporated. In 1963, he had formed a shell company known as Banco Ambrosiano Holdings SA, which began borrowing money from banks around the world which it never had any intention of repaying. A conservative estimate puts this amount at $450 million, which would make Calvi the biggest bank robber in financial history. This is a man who was included in the elite that worked with Vatican Incorporated known as "uomo di fiducia", or "men of trust."

The reason that he was able to get away with this was the good name of the Vatican Bank, with which he had associated himself. By rising to the rank of Managing Director of the priest's bank in Milan, Banco Ambrosiano, he was able to trade on the air of religiosity, which infused its reputation. Quite often, it must have looked as though he was working on behalf of the Vatican and he was not averse to using the fact that the Vatican was an independent state to put illegally purchased shares beyond the reach of the Italian Bank Inspectors.

However, after "Il Crack Sindona," money became more difficult to borrow and the share price of Ambrosiano fell dramatically, so he began to purchase his own shares at massively inflated prices, thus illegally propping up the market value. The company he used to acquire 15% of the once ailing bank was called Suprafin SA, which on paper was owned by the Vatican, but in practice was owned by Calvi himself.

In repayment for facilitating this financial fraud, he increased the Vatican deposits at Ambrosiano by 1% as well as using his Overseas branch in the Bahamian tax haven of Nassau, where Marcinkus was director, to purchase shares from the Vatican bank at grossly over-inflated amounts with money borrowed from a gullible international banking community.

He covered this up by investing in shell companies in Latin America, Nicaragua, Peru and Panama, which were beyond the jurisdiction of the Bank of Italy. Eventually, there were 17 of them in total, all owned by his Luxembourg shell company, which was in turn owned by the Vatican Bank.

Greatly overvalued shares were offered as security for huge loans, some of which were diverted to Gelli, who purchased arms for the Argentine Government in its war with Great Britain over the Falkland Islands.

Meanwhile Sindona, still fighting extradition in America, had orchestrated a blackmail campaign against his erstwhile partner-in-crime Calvi. Posters began to appear

The Falkland Islands

on the streets of Italy detailing Calvi's financial malpractice and the bank of Italy, which had been slow to move against Calvi, was spurred on to act by public outrage. Share prices in Ambrosiano dropped still further, and he was forced to hide the paper trail in an ever more convoluted path that twisted through Latin America in its efforts to stay one step ahead of the authorities.

Just when the investigators seemed on the point of establishing that Suprafin was owned by Calvi and not in fact by the Vatican, a letter appeared, signed by Luigi Mennini and the Vatican's Chief Accountant, Pellegrino de Strobel that corroborated Calvi's cover story.

In September 1978, Pope John Paul I received a list of P2 members in the "Vatican Lodge" from a news agency calling itself L'Osservatore Politico (O.P), run by a journalist called Mino Pecorelli, a former member of P2 who had fallen out with Gelli. The list which ran to over a hundred names contained many senior figures in the Vatican, including the pope's own secretary. News of his resolve to replace the Freemasons with non-Masons leaked out to Gelli and Calvi and would have been serious cause for concern. If Marckinkus were to be replaced with an honest man with no alliance to P2, the lid would be lifted on the scam that had been running so profitably for everyone involved.

Pope John Paul I was a very well-educated man from a poor rural background with a deeply spiritual nature. His desire for a return to the early days of the Church, the real wealth of which was the host of souls to whom it had brought redemption, was well documented. When he learned of the investigation into Banco Ambrosiano and the connection to the Vatican Bank, a lottery was organized among the Curia to guess which day Marcinkus would be fired.

Leo XI

At a meeting with Cardinal Villot, he made his feelings about Marcinkus clear. He was to go the following day. He also ordered the removal of Mennini, De Strobel and Monsignor de Bonis from the I.O.R.

"I wish all our links with the Banco Ambrosiano Group to be cut," he told him. "And the cut must happen in the very near future. It will be impossible, in my view, to effect this step with the present people holding the reins."

However, this plan to sweep the household clean of P2 members was not to be. For the morning after he had drawn up his list of proposed changes to the Vatican infrastructure, the Pope was found dead in his bed. He had been Pope for just thirty-three days. The last Pope to die so quickly after his election was Leo XI who had only ruled for 17 days.

The cause of death has never been established to anyone's satisfaction because no doctor would give his name to the certificate of death. Vatican officials gave the cause as heart attack due to myocardial infarction, despite the fact that this is impossible to diagnose without an autopsy and the Pope was considered to be in good health. There were growing calls from the public for an autopsy, which the Vatican refused, claiming that a Pope cannot be examined in this way, although records show that in 1830 an autopsy was performed on Pope Pius VIII.

One doctor interviewed at the time said that given the circumstances, he would not have given his consent for the body to be buried. It was remembered that the Russian Orthodox Archbishop of Leningrad had been received by the Pope only days before and had suddenly slumped forward in his chair and died. Rumors circulated that he had

Pope Pius VIII

Thomas à Kempis

There were still more deaths to come however, with Pecorelli, the former disgruntled member of P2, the next to die. Having attempted to blackmail Gelli about his involvement with the Communists, he received two bullets to the head, fired from within his mouth to indicate it was a punishment by the Sicilian Mafia for having a big mouth. Judge Emilio Allesandrini, to whom the report from the Bank of Italy's inspectors was sent asking for criminal proceedings to commence, was gunned down in the street.

The influence of P2 was such, that in an extraordinary example of corruption, the Head of Vigilance of the Bank of Italy, Mario Sarcinelli, and his Governor, Paolo Baffi, who were investigating Calvi, were actually arrested and thrown in jail, their investigation effectively curtailed. And it was not until January 1980 that the charges were dropped and proven false.

drunk a cup of coffee intended for Pope John Paul I.

Within fourteen hours of the time of death, the body had been embalmed, thus rendering impossible any investigation into the use of poison.

The nun who was accustomed to take in a cup of coffee to the Pope at 4:45 am, and who had discovered the body, asserted that he had a file of papers in his hands when she found him, despite the official version that he was reading the fifteenth century tract "The Imitation of Christ" by Thomas à Kempis. The papers, which many argue were the list of proposed changes within the Vatican, were never seen again, and the nun was packed off to a remote village in the north of Italy, far away from the media spotlight.

Mafia Boss Gaetano Badalamenti

The Vatican city

Meanwhile Marcinkus, Mennini, de Strobel and Monsignor de Bonis continued to control the Vatican Bank.

But then in 1981, Gelli's villa in Arezzo was raided by the Italian police, and a list of 962 members of P2 discovered. Suddenly, this once shadowy and powerful elite was exposed to the unwelcome glare of publicity and the resultant furore brought down the Italian Government.

The investigation into the Calvi-Marckincus-Sindona triangle of fraud was intensified and Calvi was sentenced to four years' imprisonment. If anyone doubted that P2 still had influence despite the exposure, they were silenced when Calvi lodged an appeal against his sentence, was freed on bail and then actually reinstated as the chairman of Banco Ambrosiano.

But time was running out for him. He was guilty of such serious financial fraud that he must have known there was no way out for him. He pleaded with Marcinkus to confess the involvement of the Vatican Bank with the Ambrosiano scandal. Swiss banking regulations meant that only an admission on behalf of the Vatican would reduce the enormity of his crimes. Marcinkus refused. At the time, the only charge which Calvi was facing was illegally exporting currency from Italy.

Then the letters of comfort came to light. These were letters written on the headed paper of the Instituto per le Opere di Religione, Vatican City, sent to Calvi-owned banks in Nicaragua and Peru, which were starting to balk at the amounts they had loaned with no guarantees of repayment.

Despite purporting to show the Vatican Church's assumption of the massive debts, Calvi had sent a letter to Marcinkus before the date on the letters absolving the Vatican of responsibility for the debt and thus making the letters worthless pieces of paper!

Calvi jumped bail and left Italy with a forged passport, ending up in a London hotel room. On the morning of June 17th, 1982, he was found hanging from scaffolding underneath Blackfriar's bridge with chunks of masonry in his pockets. There has been much controversy surrounding his death. Many people are convinced that he was murdered in accordance with Masonic ritual with a "cable-tow" around his neck "where the tide ebbs and flows twice in twenty-four

Blackfriar's bridge

hours." Just hours before his death, his secretary was thrown from a fourth floor window at the Banco Ambrosiano and a fake suicide note left on her desk. Another executive would go the same way a few months later.

As for Sindona, he arranged to fake his own kidnap so that he could return to Italy, armed with a copy of the "secret 500", which was a list of the exporters of black currency. The names contained therein were sufficiently powerful to guarantee the quashing of all charges against him. He also claimed that he had CIA backing for a fantastical plan to liberate Sicily from Italian control and offer it to the United States as the fifty-first state of the Union!

Gelli was caught out when he emerged from hiding in South America to arrange the transfer of $55 million from one of his secret Swiss bank accounts to an account in Uruguay. Told that he would have to appear in person to effect the transfer, he was immediately arrested. However, he managed to escape prison while awaiting extradition and was helped to Monte Carlo by his many friends in high places. A yacht was placed at his disposal and he returned to Uruguay having "apologized" for escaping and recommending that the guard who helped him be treated leniently!

Marcinkus lived out the rest of his days within the confines of the Vatican walls where he could not be touched by the Italian authorities. The Curia would not even accept the papers that the state prosecutors attempted to serve on him and others in the I.O.R.

As for the continued existence of Masonic lodge P2, one should not underestimate a secret society that included amongst its number, three members of Cabinet, (of which one was the Justice Minister), several former Prime Ministers, forty-three members of Parliament and over one hundred top officials in the Vatican. Although largely broken up, the chairman of the commission appointed to investigate it, warned,

"P2 is by no means dead. It still has power. It is working in the institutions. It is moving in society. It has money, means and instruments still at its disposal. It still has fully operative power centers in South America. It is also still able to condition, at least in part, Italian political life."

FOUNDER OF OPUS DEI

chapter 9

ONE ORGANIZATION WHICH MUST RUE THE PUBLICATION OF DAN BROWN'S BLOCKBUSTER NOVEL "THE DA VINCI CODE" IS OPUS DEI. WITH ITS PORTRAYAL OF THE RUTHLESS PRESIDENT-GENERAL BISHOP MANUEL ARINGAROSSA AND SILAS, THE HOMICIDAL SELF-FLAGELLATING ALBINO MONK, IT DOES PRESENT A RATHER ONE-DIMENSIONAL AND SENSATIONAL PICTURE OF THIS CATHOLIC INSTITUTION.

Opus

Virgin Mary

However there are those both within and without the Catholic Church who have expressed grave concerns about the practices of Opus Dei, especially the way it targets new recruits.

Leaving aside for a moment an ethical consideration of their methods, one has only to mention their global headquarters to be greeted with raised eyebrows and looks of disbelief. Situated in the heart of Manhattan at 243 Lexington Avenue, the 133,000 square foot tower is a prime piece of real estate estimated to be worth nearly $50 million. With over a hundred bedrooms, chapels, dining rooms, conference halls and offices, furnished in immaculate marble and clad in Indiana limestone, it is a most impressive building, and a far cry from Opus Dei's humble beginnings.

The father of Opus Dei was a Spanish priest named Josemaria Escriva. Plagued by illness as a young child, he was once so close to death that his mother took him to a popular shrine of the Virgin Mary at Torreciudad and prayed for him. He did indeed make a remarkable recovery, and when his mother related this incident to him, it made a great impression upon him. He began to believe that God had spared his life for a reason.

Like many young men at the time he decided on a career in the Church, combining his ecclesiastical studies with a degree in law. An intelligent and good-looking young man he stood out at his seminary because of the fastidious care he took with his appearance.

On October 2nd, 1928 the idea to found Opus Dei came to him "like a divine seed falling from heaven" but the first few years were fraught with the social upheaval and civil strife which was to plague Spain in the years surrounding the civil war.

Teaching in Spanish universities had become increasingly secular and the increasing trend towards agnosticism amongst the up and coming Spanish intellectuals caused a backlash from the ultra conservative Spanish elite, wedded to the traditional power bases of the Church and Crown.

When a republic was proclaimed in 1931, the forces of agnosticism and socialism seemed to have won the day. Monasteries and churches were burnt and the Jesuits expelled from Spain. Crucifixes were no longer permitted anywhere near schools, Church property was taken over by the State and the relationship between Spain and the Vatican set out in the Concordat was terminated.

In this challenging climate, Escriva began to hold regular meetings with a group of like-minded men and women and was eventually able to purchase a property,

Saint Ignatius Loyola, Founder of Society of Jesus

which acted as both residence and educational academy. Meanwhile, he began work on his collection of maxims (999 in total) called El Camino or The Way, first published in 1934.

In July 1936, Madrid fell to the Republicans and Escriva had to go into hiding as his life would have been in considerable danger had he been caught in his clerical garb. Over 6,000 priests were killed in the course of the Spanish Civil War and Escriva had to dress in the boiler suit of a manual worker to avoid attracting attention from the Republican troops thronging the city.

He spent the next two weeks hiding out at his mother's flat until he was tipped off that the building was about to be searched and with the militia entering through the front, he slipped out the back, his tonsure concealed under a hat, a wedding ring on his finger to complete the disguise.

At one point, he was forced to hide in a psychiatric hospital, pretending to be mentally ill and he eventually found a safe house in the Honduran Embassy, who supplied him with a certificate of employment so he could provide identity papers if challenged. But the constant danger of arrest prompted him to leave the Republican-occupied side of Spain, travelling incognito up towards the border, even camping out in the woods to escape detection by the frontier guards. Once in France, he made plans to return to the nationalist side of the front line.

When the nationalist troops marched triumphantly into Madrid in 1939, he returned to find his academy in ruins. But in the post-war years, Opus Dei's expansion was very rapid indeed. As a reaction against the liberal anti-Catholic stance of the socialists, the religion of Spain under Franco was National Catholicism, by which is meant a mixture of religion and patriotic fervor, extremely intolerant of anything it deemed "other", by which was meant Protestantism, Liberalism, Socialism, Judaism and so on.

As is clear from El Camino, Escriva was a vocal adherent of National Catholicism, equating the salvation of one's soul with the salvation of Spain: "If these maxims change your own life, you will be a perfect imitator of Jesus Christ, and a knight without spot. And with Christs such as you, Spain will return to the ancient grandeur of its saints, its sages and its heroes."

Scientific research was taken out of the hands of the "godless" and religious education became mandatory, not just for students at school but those at university as well. Halls of Residence were established under the control of members of religious orders who enforced strict codes of moral discipline.

In charge of the program of Educational Reform was Jose Ibanez Martin, a close friend of Opus Dei member Jose Maria Albareda Herrera, whom he named vice president of the program. Over the succeeding years, a good many Opus members came to fill the university positions left open after the civil war. They were deemed safe candidates, ideologically sound with guaranteed affiliations to Church and State.

Opposition to Opus Dei's growing influence soon began to assert itself, especially in cities that had been opposed to Franco during the war. In Barcelona copies of El Camino were burnt and an intense rivalry with the Jesuits began to emerge. One ex-member, Maria del Carmen Tapia, who wrote a book about her experiences in Opus Dei, claimed that Escriva had said it would be better to die unshriven than to receive the last rites from the hands of a Jesuit!

At one point, Opus Dei was even accused of being a Jewish sect controlled by Freemasons, which was a serious allegation in Franco's Spain and representatives had to appear before a tribunal to answer the charge.

One charge still levelled at Opus Dei is that of obstructive secrecy. Although this has been explained as rather a "reserve" on the part of its members and an antidote to pride, it is an accusation, which has crystallized in the public consciousness. The Constitution, which lays down the rules of Opus Dei, is notoriously difficult to get hold of, and indeed is only available in Latin.

When James Martin, associate editor of the Catholic magazine America and a priest at St. Ignatius Loyola Church in Manhattan asked Opus Dei (communications) director Bill Schmidt why the Constitutions had never been translated into English, he was told that this was because it was a Church-owned document owned by the Holy See who did not want it translated.

On verifying this with three experts in canon law he found this was unprecedented, that there was in fact "no general ecclesiastical prohibition against the translation of documents of religious orders." The inevitable conclusion was that it was Opus Dei and not the Holy See, which had prevented the translation of the documents.

Javier Echevarria Opus Dei's Prelate Bishop

Maria del Carmen Tapia, despite being the head of the women's section of Opus Dei in Venezuela was only allowed to consult the document for brief periods at a time under the watchful eye of the archivist. And Ann Schweniger, another former member, confirmed that the only document made available was the catechism, which was kept under lock and key, only open to study under strict supervision and even then she was told to make her notes in code so that they would inscrutable to non-members.

Responding to the accusation of secrecy in an interview in 1966, Escriva had replied that "Any reasonably well-informed person knows that there is nothing secret about Opus Dei. It is easy to get to know Opus Dei. It works in broad daylight in all countries, with the full juridical recognition of the civil and ecclesiastical authorities. The names of its directors and of its apostolic undertakings are well-known. Anyone who wants information can obtain it without difficulty."

However, despite his rebuttal, the Constitution makes explicit injunctions that members of Opus Dei cannot

Saint Josemaria Escriva

Vatican City

disclose their membership without permission, nor can they reveal the names of their fellow members, especially any that have left for one reason or another. No special insignia is to be worn which could identify members and there is to be no public display of membership, such as taking part in a church procession. Discussing Opus Dei with non-members is also forbidden.

The policy also exists of withholding the full version of the Constitution from the local bishop in whose diocese Opus Dei wished to open a center and only making available a summary.

Another accusation levelled at Opus Dei concerns the way it targets new recruits. Father Andrew Byrne was quoted in the Daily Mail in January 1981 as saying:

"In some cases when a youngster says he wants to join, we do advise them not to tell their parents. This is because the parents do not understand us."

It is the duty of every member of Opus Dei to win converts. "Fishing", as it is known, can take place anywhere, such as the work place although Catholic run schools and halls of residence at universities have become established recruiting grounds. One headmistress was forced to ban Opus Dei from the premises after students were attending unauthorized meetings with an Opus Dei priest on the lawn. In another case, a student complained to the head of his college, that he was being harassed by Opus members despite professing no interest in joining their organization.

Many of the Opus Dei properties have youth clubs attached to them and alongside recreational activities, lectures and discussion groups are held, at which those considered to have a vocation are encouraged to pursue a

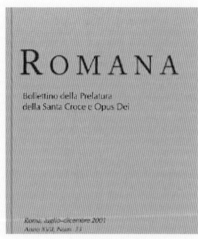

The official bulletin of the Prelature of Opus Dei

more spiritual line in their studies. There have also been complaints that a sense of dependency on Opus Dei was gradually and deliberately built up as the following directive suggests:

"To direct this growth, there is the talk with the priest and conversation which each youngster has with whomever is working with him, in order to tell, in the confidence of a younger brother, their little secrets and worries of all kinds. In the beginning it is difficult for them. Afterwards they need it."

The most promising candidates are rewarded with an annual Easter pilgrimage to Rome and the feeling that they are part of an elite group is deliberately fostered. One disgruntled ex-member told The Catholic

Canonization of St. Josemaria

Pictorial, a Liverpool weekly in 1981, "By the time you've gone on the Easter pilgrimage, you're just begging to join."

Often a potential recruit will be befriended and then introduced to a wider circle of Opus members. Once they are in that circle, the friendship, which was a means of recruitment, will fade away as the professionals take over.

University campuses are particularly attractive to Opus Dei as recruiting grounds, as they make no bones of their desire to attract members from the well-educated classes, indeed Rule 116 of the Constitutions explicitly states that intellectuals and those who have reached high office are to be sought out because of their influence in civil society.

This, combined with the desire to catch them young, makes the campus especially fertile soil. One of the many complaints aimed at Opus Dei by students is that they are not made aware of the exact nature of what they are getting involved in. One student thought he had joined some kind of informal discussion group or think tank. He was even unaware that some of his peers were taking vows of celibacy. Asking awkward question at his next meeting about the role of women and the lack of ethnic minorities, he was asked not to return and his friendship with the man who had originally introduced him was effectively finished.

The next stage will be what ex-members refer to as a "vocation crisis". The recruit will be told that now is the time to make the commitment to Opus Dei, that God has given him this opportunity and he must take it or he may put himself beyond God's Grace for the rest of his life. This is rather like the salesman clicking his ballpoint pen and pointing at the dotted line to close the deal.

Disturbingly, for an organization which prides itself on the intellectual tenor of its members, once a student has been assigned a spiritual director, a concerted effort is undertaken to monitor his studies. As well as checking his or her mail, the director has to approve the classes and the reading material. In one case, a student reading politics was told to avoid direct contact with the Marxist texts and instead approach them through Opus Dei's commentaries.

This chimes with Maxim 339 of Escriva's El Camino:

"Books: don't buy them without advice from a Catholic who is learned or prudent. It is easy to buy something useless or harmful. How often a man thinks he is carrying a book under his arm, and it turns out to be a load of dirt!"

John Paul II ordaining the first Opus Dei prelate, Bishop Alvaro del Portillo

Once a young candidate has joined Opus Dei, relations with non-members, even close family, are frowned upon and in some cases actively discouraged. This is particularly true when it comes to questions of attendance at family events such as weddings and baptisms. In one instance the fear of old family bonds being reawakened prompted

The calling of St Mathew, Caravaggio

Opus Dei to refuse permission for a young member to be a bridesmaid at her sister's wedding, at which point she decided to leave.

This tendency to bypass parental approval is what has caused the most consternation. There is nothing wrong per se with a young person wishing to join a religious order. Although it is becoming rarer in our increasingly secular age, many young people no doubt feel a genuine calling, but they should not be rushed into making decisions, such as vows of celibacy, which could affect the rest of their lives. If they are below the age, their parents' wishes must be respected, even if absolute consent is not needed, for although no one is admitted to Opus Dei before the age of eighteen, the process of recruitment may be well under way by then.

Dianne DiNicola is a parent who was so concerned about Opus Dei's activities that in 1991, she started the Opus Dei Awareness Network (ODAN), an outreach support group for families with children in Opus Dei. When her daughter, Tammy, an undergraduate at Boston college became increasingly "cold and secretive" and finally wrote a letter saying she was living as a numerary in an Opus Dei center in Boston and would not be returning home, Dianne hired an "exit counsellor" in frustration at the lack of help available from the Church.

On the pretext of inviting Tammy home for her graduation, she was able to engineer a meeting with the counsellor and at the end of a tumultuous 24-hour session, Tammy decided to leave. Diane later found out that this was the last time Tammy was to return home as she had been told by Opus Dei to sever contact with her family.

Opus Dei is highly critical of ODAN, describing members who have been exited in this way as having been 'violated'. Such reluctance to lose new recruits is understandable in any organization but is taken to extremes with Opus Dei, as in the case of the father who met up

Work of Opus Dei
"Be a saint through your work".

with his daughter, also a numerary. She decided to accompany him home for an impromptu visit, only to have a superior telephone the house and accuse the father of kidnapping his own daughter!

And it is not just over-protective and over-emotional parents who are concerned with their children's involvement with Opus Dei. As long ago as 1981 the Archbishop of Westminster, Cardinal Hume, was moved to write an article in the Times in which he set out guidelines for the activities of Opus Dei within his diocese:

"I now wish to make public these four recommendations. Each of them arises from one fundamental principle: that the procedures and activities of an international movement, present in a particular diocese, may well have to be modified prudently in the light of the cultural differences and legitimate local customs and standards of the society within which that international body seeks to work.

1. No person under eighteen years of age should be allowed to take any vow or long-term commitment in association with Opus Dei.

2. It is essential that young people who wish to join Opus Dei should first discuss the matter with their parents or legal guardians. If there are, by exception, good reasons for not approaching their families, these reasons should, in every case, be discussed with the local bishop or his delegate.

3. While it is accepted that those who join Opus Dei take on the proper duties and responsibilities of membership, care must be taken to respect the freedom of the individual; first, the freedom of the individual to join or to leave the organization without undue pressure being exerted; secondly, the freedom of the individual at any stage to choose his or her own spiritual director, whether or not

the director is a member of Opus Dei.

4. Initiatives and activities of Opus Dei, within the diocese of Westminster, should carry a clear indication of their sponsorship and management.

Surprisingly, given the detailed description of the Cardinal's wishes, one young member of Opus Dei, on asking why they were not being respected, was told that since they were guidelines only and not rules, Opus Dei was under no obligation to carry them out.

For those who do leave Opus Dei, they often find that their troubles are only just beginning. Adjusting to life in the outside world after the closeted existence within the organization can be hard. This is especially true because many members are made to believe that by leaving they are putting their own personal salvation in jeopardy.

In the same way that many Christians believe that their is the only sure way to Heaven, members of Opus are taught to believe that in fact the gates to Heaven can only be reached with absolute certainty by following El Camino or the Road laid out by their founding father, Josemaria Escriva.

This may go some way towards explaining the zealous efforts at conversion, in that it is a genuinely felt mission to save as many souls as possible. In his work "The Inner World of Opus Dei", John Roche wrote that each member should try to cultivate at least fifteen friends with "potential", and at anyone time he should be working directly to win over five of them.

By staking a claim to the toll-gate on the route to salvation, Opus Dei harks back, as ex-member Raimundo Pannikar describes it, to "the last remnant of that militant messianism which is endemic in the Abrahamic religions" by which he means Judaism, Christianity and Islam, all of

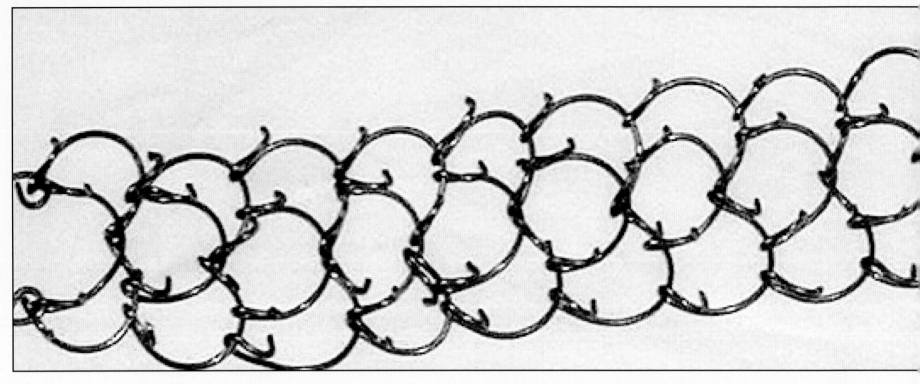

at regular intervals all of these religions throw up groups, which claim to represent the original pure faith that has been diluted by the encroaching influence of secular society.

In the Opus Dei journal Cronica, Escriva goes so far as to say,

"As I have not ceased to warn you, the evil comes from within [the Church] and from very high up. There is an authentic rottenness, and at times it seems as if the Mystical Body of Christ were a corpse in decomposition, that it stinks... Ask forgiveness, my children, for these contemptible actions which are made possible in the Church and from above, corrupting souls almost from infancy."

In Maria Angustias Moreno's book "El Opus Dei: Anexo a una Historia" she quotes an Opus priest as saying,

"We are the remnant of the people of Israel. We are the only ones, who, having remained faithful to God, can still save the Church today. Given the state of the Church today, it seems as if it were abandoned by the Holy Spirit. We are the ones who can save the Church by our faithfulness to the Father."

The confessional is also jealously guarded and Opus members are actively discouraged from confessing to non-Opus priests. Although the Rules state that in accordance with Canon Law, a member may go for his weekly confession to any episcopally-approved priest of his choosing, with no need to provide an account to an Opus superior, in practice this is virtually unheard of. And in Cronica Escriva makes plain his feelings regarding clergy outside Opus Dei:

"All my children have freedom to go to confession with any priest approved by the Ordinary and they are not obliged to tell the directors of the Work what they have done. Does a person who does this sin? No! Does he have a good spirit? No! He is on the way to listening to the advice of bad shepherds...

"You will go to your brothers the priests as I do. And to them you will open wide your hearts with sincerity, rotten if it were rotten, with a deep desire to cure yourself. If not, that rottenness would never be cured... and doing

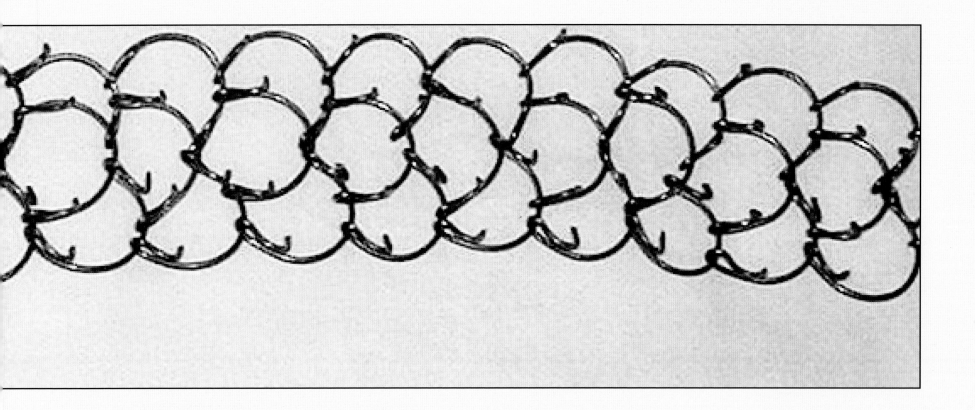

this wrong, seeking a second-hand doctor who cannot give us more than a few seconds of his time...we would also harm the Work. If you were to do this you'd have the wrong spirit, you'd be unhappy. You wouldn't sin because of this, but woe to you! You would have begun to err."

This concern with keeping confession within the ranks of Opus Dei seems almost to become an instrument of control over its members. Vladimir Felzmann, a vocal ex-member of Opus Dei, relates how he was castigated by senior officials for not sending word to Rome of a member who confessed to homosexual feelings. They had somehow got wind of it and answered his protestations about the confidential seal of the confessional by rebuking him for not having urged the member to admit his sin in another context, which would have allowed the information to be used.

The Rules also state that "each week all members must talk familiarly and in confidence with the local Director, so that a better apostolic activity may be organized and encouraged."

This practice, known in Opus Dei as "the confidence", was once undertaken two or three times a year by religious orders but since there was no protection of the "seal of the confessional" it was open to abuse and was banned by the Catholic Church in 1890. Its importance to Opus Dei is such that it is variously described as a "pious custom" and "devout obligation" and is supposed to ensure that nothing is hid from the superiors, which could be an obstacle to salvation.

Prelatic Church of Opus Dei at
the Opus Dei headquarters in Rome

It is combined with "the circle", also known as "the chapter of faults", which can be likened to a public confession, in which members gather round and accuse first themselves and then their brethren. Although similar to many group therapy sessions, it takes place without the presence of a trained therapist and can be a very humiliating experience. Once again, this practice is open to abuse as the information freely divulged may come back to haunt the confessor.

When salvation is taught to stem from the grace of the founding father, taking the step of cutting oneself off from that grace, can seem like laying oneself open to eternal damnation. The feeling of spiritual isolation is compounded by the fact that members are not allowed to contact non-members and very often all familial ties have been broken at a relatively young age.

One accusatory voice goes so far as to maintain that there has been a deliberate attempt to blur the boundary between the will of Escriva and the will of God when it is sometimes left unclear who is being described by the words "Our Father." When urged to surrender one's will to the father, it can be read that Escriva's will should be followed unquestioningly. When this is combined with a way of life which is closely regulated and cut off from people who hold different views, it can be appreciated how potentially disastrous a crisis of conscience would be for a member.

Time and time again absolute obedience to the precepts of El Camino is exhorted as in "Filial fear is the gateway to love", "In our docility there will be no limits" or the warning against the "sterile and false independence... that leaves a man in darkness when it abandons him to his own judgement."

Another criticism levelled at Opus Dei is in its treatment of women. Despite the 1917 Code of Canon Law which states that female religious orders should have their own superiors and not depend for government on their male equivalents, this is clearly not the case with Opus Dei, where regional authority resides with male regional counsellors and the ultimate authority also lies within the hands of the male successors to Escriva.

In maxim 946, he claims that "women needn't be scholars, it's enough for them to be prudent." And whereas the prayer which closes meetings in the male branch runs thus: "Holy Mary, Our Hope, Seat of Wisdom, pray for us" the prayer that women are expected to use is: "Holy Mary, Our Hope, Handmaid of the Lord, pray for us." The implication is that wisdom is not expected as a feminine attribute and the reference to handmaid (female servant) points to the role they are to play within Opus Dei.

Although from the outset women were involved with running schools for girls, preparing domestic servants for work, and working in Christian bookshops and libraries, it was also made abundantly clear that the rather more mundane tasks involved in the day-to-day management of

Pope John Paul II called Opus Dei's founder,
"the Saint of Ordinary Life"

INDEX LIBRORVM
PROHIBITORVM,

CVM REGVLIS CONFECTIS
per Patres a Tridentina Synodo delectos,
auctoritate Sanctiss. D.N. Pij IIII,
Pont. Max. comprobatus.

VENETIIS, M. D. LXIIII.

According to ex members, Opus Dei maintains an
"Index of forbidden books[1]" based on the list used by
the Roman Catholic Church until 1966

Freemasonry in the 18th century

mundane tasks involved in the day-to-day management of the institute's houses, such as cooking and cleaning, were to be left to them. This was however to be accomplished without the temptations of the flesh that should arise were mean and women to mix, hence the need for separate entrances which effectively turn one institute into two. At Netherhall House in Hampstead, London, double doors separate the sexes and each night they are ritually locked.

There are a confusing number of grades and divisions within the hierarchy of Opus Dei, something which other religious orders have increasingly done away with because they interfere with community life. One thing they are all expected to practice however is corporal mortification.

Paragraph 260 of the 1950 Constitution states that:

"The pious custom of chastising the body and reducing it to servitude by wearing a small cilice for at least two hours a day, by taking the discipline at least once a week, and by sleeping on the ground, will be faithfully maintained, taking into account only a person's health."

The Catholic Pictorial in 1981 described a routine of kissing the floor upon being awoken by the early morning knock, taking cold showers, observing the "great silence" in effect since the previous evening's prayers until after breakfast and then the "lesser silence" for a shorter duration before lunchtime. The spiked chain was to be worn around the leg or the arm for two hours at a time except Feast Days and Sundays and once a week a rope whip was applied to the buttocks.

Opus Dei have good reason to complain of their sensational and one-sided portrayal in Dan Brown's "The Da Vinci Code". No one is suggesting for a minute that they would ever sanction murder to preserve the status quo of a male-dominated power base within the Catholic Church. However as regards the self-flagellating monk, Silas, there are undoubted parallels to be drawn.

At a time when this practice has fallen into disrepute among other religious orders because of the unhealthy masochism it promotes, it seems to be a matter of pride with Opus Dei that its founding father not only designed his own discipline, fashioning a cat-o'-nine-tails with shards of metal and razor blades, but that he beat himself so severely, the walls were spattered with blood.

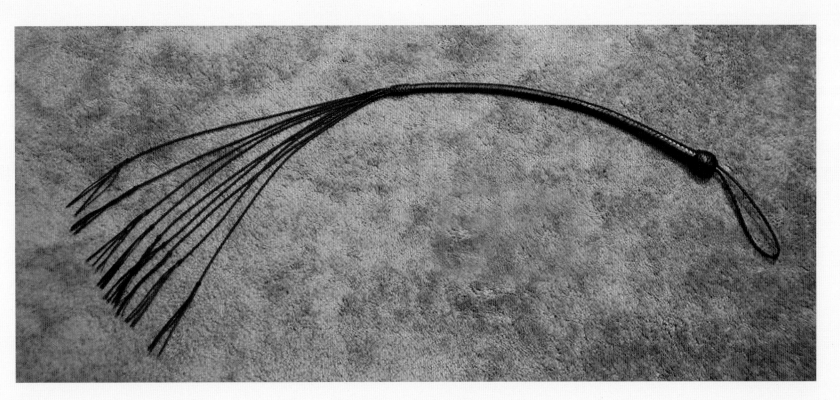

Cat-o-nine-tails

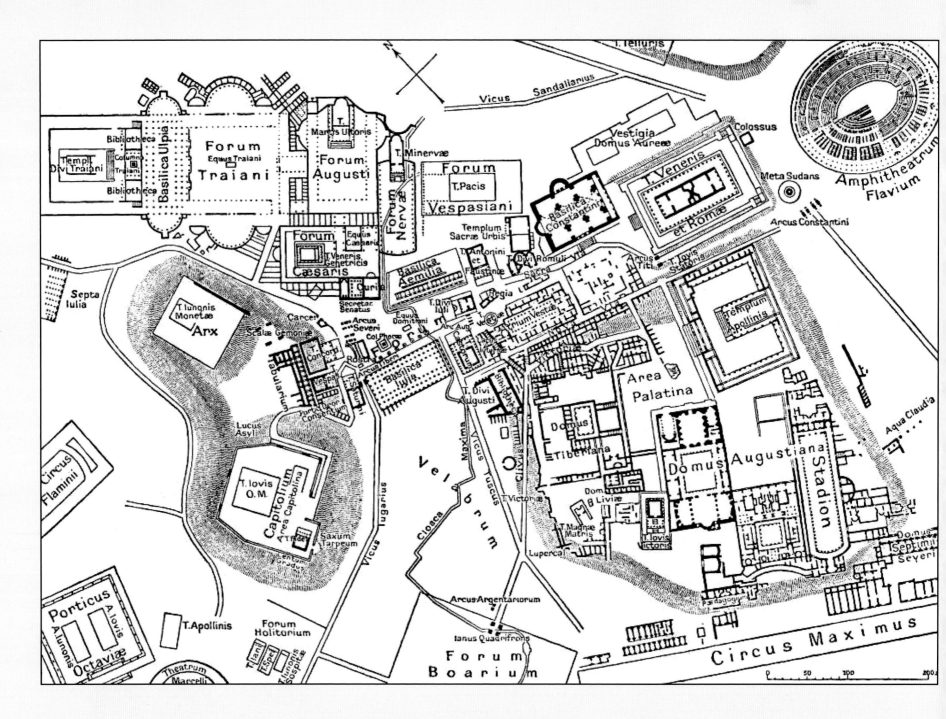

A map of central Rome during the Roman Empire